11.00

FAO FISHING MANUALS

MENDING OF FISHING NETS

D0813389

FAO Fishing Manuals

Mending of fishing nets

L. Libert and A. Maucorps

Published by arrangement with the
Food and Agriculture Organization of the United Nations
by **Fishing News Books Ltd**
1 Long Garden Walk, Farnham
Surrey, England

First published 1973
Reprinted 1978
Reprinted 1981

ISBN 0 85238 062 3

Printed in England by
Adlard & Son Ltd
Bartholomew Press
Dorking, Surrey

CONTENTS

LIST OF FIGURES

AN INTRODUCTORY NOTE

This manual on mending of fishing nets is the translation of Le Ramendage des Filets de Pêche by L. Libert and A. Maucorps of the French Institute of Sea Fisheries (Institut Scientifique et Technique des Pêches Maritimes), published in *Revue des travaux de l'ISTPM*, fasc. 2, Juin 1968. The Food and Agriculture Organization of the United Nations is indebted to the authors and Dr. C. Maurin, Director of this Institute, for their gracious permission to publish this English edition in the series of FAO Fishing Manuals.

The work of Messrs. Libert and Maucorps was selected by FAO from among many other publications on the same subject because of its outstanding didactic quality in describing and illustrating the whole subject of net mending operations, which makes it particularly valuable for teaching and training purposes. The English edition will broaden the audience of this valuable teaching aid, particularly for the promotion of developing fisheries.

The manual was translated in the FAO Translation Service and technically edited in the Fishery Industries Division.

CHAPTER 1

1. Introduction

Net mending is the repairing of fishing nets that have been damaged and this may be done either on board or in workshops ashore.

Among the subjects dealt with in books on fishing nets published in France to date, the mending of nets has been dealt with only very superficially, no doubt because of its apparent simplicity where straight nets are involved. However, with the development of trawling and new types of gear, the difficulties of net repair have increased appreciably. These difficulties which have to be solved by the netmakers workshops or the fishermen themselves, sometimes pose problems which are noted not only in current operation but also in training courses for young mates and skippers. This manual on net mending was initially started to assist as far as possible to solve these problems. In order to make it accessible to the largest range from amateur, student, to trainee and also to qualified fishermen, the same methodological order in the description of the various operations was followed which was adopted for the 22-lesson course on net mending given for instructors in this subject in seamen's apprenticeship schools.

It is moreover hoped that the techniques described in this manual, which pertains specifically to trawls, as for instance, how to make double selvedges and corners of squares, will be useful for the standardization of working methods in workshops.

CHAPTER 2

MATERIALS USED AND GENERAL CONCEPTS

2.1 Materials used in the workshop

The ordinary outfit of a workshop consists of the braiding rod on the trestle, hooks for the attachment of netting sheets or net sections to be mended, twine bobbins, spools, net braiding needles, a pair of scissors and a knife.

The best set-up is one where all these materials are placed within easy reach.

2.1.1. THE TRESTLE

For working separate pieces, the best device in our view is a wooden trestle from 2 to 2,50 m long and 1,20 to 1,50 m high (Figure 1).

On this trestle there should be:

— a braiding rod, consisting of a cylindrical iron bar firmly fitted so that

FIGURE 1.—Trestle. A piece of netting, that is to become the headpiece, hangs on the metal bar.

it will not move on screw hooks set about 5 cm from the upper edge;
— a set of round iron rods inserted in the upper portion used as unwinding axes for the twine bobbins, or as points for hanging the panel being mended and
— a rack for keeping the needles, meshsticks and knife, at mid-height in the open space between the legs of the trestle.

2.1.2 THE TWINES

Netting sections, e.g. of trawl nets, are made of twines of different specification (strength, and possibly, construction). The same is true for the coloured twine used to make joins.

2.1.3 THE MESHSTICK

The meshstick is indispensable in continuous hand braiding. It is made of a piece of hard smooth wood, either flat or rounded, about 10 cm long. Its cross-section, which varies with size of the mesh of the net being made, is equal to the length of two sides of the mesh laced on it. In cross-section it may be either rectangular (Figure 2F) round, or even oval shaped (Figure

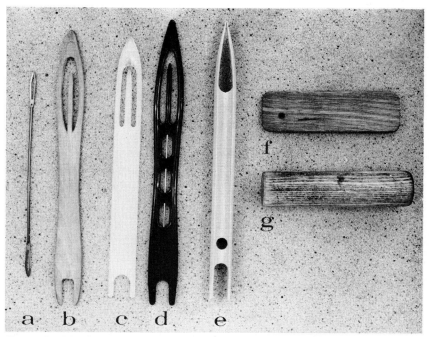

FIGURE 2.—Needles and meshsticks. A—metal needle for small meshsizes; B—wooden needle or the usual model; C—plastic needle of the same shape as B; D—reinforced plastic needle; E—plastic needle without tongue; F and G—wooden meshsticks, one rectangular and the other round.

2G). The choice between these two types of meshstick depends on local custom and often even on the region or port in question. However, the flat meshstick seems best suited for trawl net mending.

Each meshstick is numbered, according to the meshsize it makes. Thus in braiding with a No. 10 meshstick, the meshes are 10 cm long, i.e. 5 cm for each bar.

During mending, the meshstick is used in the workshop when several meshes are to be braided or when it is difficult to work without a meshstick, for instance in mending netting sections with very small or very large meshes.

2.1.4   THE NEEDLE

In fishermen's language the needle is the instrument that holds the twine necessary for work on netting. It may be made of wood, bone, plastic or metal and comes in various shapes (Figure 2); here we shall discuss only those most commonly used.

The metal needle (Figure 2A) is particularly suited to work on meshes less than 10 mm in size. For larger ones, the conventional type needle is used (Figure 2B, C, and D), of a convenient dimension for the size of the meshes to be made.

The plastic needle (Figure 2E), without a tongue but with the fore portion open has an additional advantage of permitting machine refilling. Some of these needles are designated by a number varying with the manufacture. For instance, for those made of wood, No. 1 is the smallest and No. 5 the largest; for reinforced plastic needles, No. 0 is the largest and No. 16 the smallest.

2.2
General Concepts: The headpiece, definitions, knots

2.2.1   THE HEADPIECE

In hand braiding the first rows of a piece of webbing or netting section are attached to a headpiece (or set-up). It consists of either a piece of netting

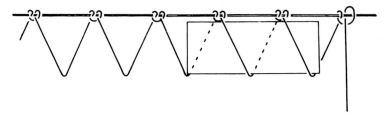

FIGURE 3.—Heading (or set-up) twine. Making the first row with the help of a meshstick.

several meshes deep and of sufficient width or breadth for this purpose, or else a horizontally stretched length of twine on which the first row is attached by clove-hitches (Figure 3). In the first instance, the initial row, that will be lost when the piece of netting is detached from the headpiece, is made of poorer quality twine. In the second instance, in order to start the work on the braiding rod, the first row is freed by drawing the twine used for set-up as soon as several rows of meshes have been braided.

2.2.2 DEFINITIONS

The *direction of the netting* is given by the direction of the force parallel to the diagonal of the mesh, which tends to tighten the knots while keeping them in the correct position.

The *direction of braiding* is that parallel to the general course of the rows, as formed during braiding by hand; it is perpendicular to the direction of the netting and corresponds to the general run of the twine.

A *row* is a series of loops or half-meshes, aligned in the direction of braiding; it is one half-mesh in height. Accordingly two successive rows have to be braided to increase the depth of a panel by one mesh.

The dimensions of a netting panel are expressed in number of meshes, counted in the direction of braiding (which is also the general direction of the twine) for width and in the direction of the netting for depth.

Along the edges, as well as in the inner portion of a suspended panel, the direction of the netting being vertical, there is a free corner either on the top or on the bottom of any mesh, called a mesh or cleaned mesh.

If the free corner is located either to the right or the left of the mesh, it is called a point or side mesh; it always has one knot which, contrary to the one in the cleaned mesh, cannot be undone without destroying the mesh (cut meshes).

A cut parallel to the sides of the mesh forms a bar at each knot connecting three sides of the mesh.

It should be pointed out that the International Organization for Standardization (ISO) recommends the use of the following symbols for the various types of cut.

> T = transversal or horizontal cut, with cleaned meshes
> N = normal or vertical cut, with points
> B = cut on the bias, with bars.

2.2.3 KNOTS USED IN MENDING

The *sheet bend*, or weaver's knot, is the most common type of knot used on cleaned meshes in normal braiding.

The *double sheet bend* is generally used only at the beginning and at the ends of tears being repaired, on the starting or end bars. It is also used instead of the sheet bend when the net is braided with a double knot, as for certain types of netting made of very fine nylon thread.

The *single fisherman's knot* is used to tie up twines of needles used one after another in the course of the work. Because of its excellent grip it is recommended particularly for synthetic twine. The above-mentioned sheet bend is also used sometimes for such connections.

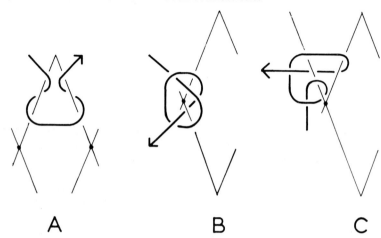

A   **B**   **C**

FIGURE 4.—Replacement knots. A—flat knot; B—overhand knot; C—two half-hitches.

The *side knot*, special for mending purposes, is used only on points.

The *overhand knot* is used in certain types of mending to mark the point.

An explanation of how these various knots are tied is given in the description of the operations of braiding and mending.

For the record we mention the frequent use during net mending on board ship, instead of the above-described knots, of the following kinds of knot that generally hold well:

— the *square knot* instead of the single sheet bent on the cleaned meshes to be picked up (Figure 4A);

— the *overhand knot*, instead of the side knot (Figure 4B);

— and *two half hitches* instead of the double sheet bend (Figure 4C).

CHAPTER 3

3.   **CUTTING**

Nets are cut with either a knife or scissors or even, for synthetic twine, with a hot iron in the workshop. The purpose is to make side meshes, (i.e. points) cleaned meshes and bars.

In order to insert patches inside pieces of netting, as in mending proper, all types of cut are usual. We shall now describe how different types of regular cuts are made along the sides of pieces and then explain how in braiding by hand various types of selvedges are obtained with bating (loss of meshes) or creasing (gaining of meshes) to shape the net. The cuts formed by irregular alternation of points, meshes and bars in preparation for repairing of tears are described in the chapter on net mending.

3.1   Materials used

In order to illustrate cuts, the netting used, which has a bar length of about 40 mm in actual size, here on the designs usually reduced to 10 mm, is hung on the hooks of the trestle in such a way that the direction of the netting is perpendicular to the braiding rod.

3.2   Cutting of a rectangular piece of netting

Any rectangular-shaped piece is obtained on the one hand by two all-meshes cuts, the one to give the initial width and the other to delimit the depth, and on the other hand by two all-points cuts to keep the width the same at all levels (Figure 5).

The following example will illustrate how two such cuts are made, beginning with an all-meshes cut at the bottom of the panel.

3.2.1   ALL-MESHES CUTTING PATTERN

The reader is reminded that this cut is made perpendicular to the direction of the netting (Figure 5a).

In order to obtain the first mesh, the two sides of the mesh at the *base* of any knot whatsoever in the inside of the net are cut. This cut is repeated at the *base* of all the knots to the right and along the same level as the

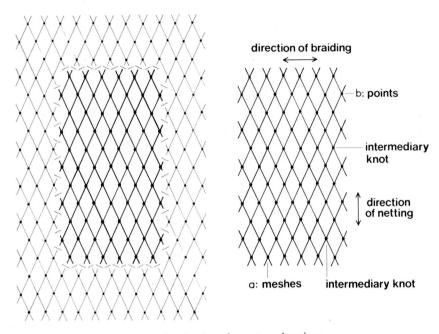

FIGURE 5.—Cutting of a rectangular piece.

initial one. This gives a series of meshes between which one locates a knot, like any other knot in the piece of netting, connecting four mesh sides. In the cut that follows a similar knot will also be found in all spaces between the points. When this knot is on the edge of a piece, of a tear or of a hole, we call it the *intermediary knot* to distinguish it both from the other knots of the net that are not along the edge and from the knots connecting two or three mesh sides.

3.2.2 ALL-POINTS CUTTING PATTERN

This cut is made parallel to the direction of the netting (Figure 5b).

Here we will begin on the right side, starting with the intermediary knot located to the right of the last mesh cut. One or two fingers are inserted into the last mesh, that is to be released on the right side so that it becomes a corner angle; the first point is formed by cutting the two sides of the mesh to the right of the said intermediary knot; then, the other points are obtained by repeating the same cut each time to the right of the second intermediary knots one comes across moving in the direction of the cut.

3.2.3. COMPLETION OF THE CUTTING OF THE RECTANGULAR PIECE OF NETTING

If a piece is being taken out of a net, the cut is usually continued along one side after the other, following the contour. The above-described procedure differs very little from the usual method, the idea being to specify how the points on the left side are obtained starting from the same base as for those on the right side.

After having counted the desired number of meshes along the bottom row, the first point on the left side is obtained by cutting the two sides of the meshes to the left of the intermediary knot coming after the last mesh counted; the next points are obtained in this same way, by repeating the said cut again and again to the left of the second intermediary knot one comes across moving in the direction of the cut.

Once the same number of points has been obtained on each side edge, the cutting of the rectangular piece is completed by working either from the left or from the right.

The first mesh is obtained by cutting the two sides of the mesh located above the intermediary knot following the last point formed; the cut is then continued on top of all the knots along the same level as the first mesh.

When the last mesh is snipped the desired small rectangular piece is separated from the rest of the net.

These two cutting techniques, one involving meshes and the other points, are also called right-hand cuts, the first in width and the second in depth.

3.3 Oblique cuts

Generally speaking trapezoid or triangular-shaped pieces of netting are obtained by working along the side edges. At least, one of these edges is cut differently from the all-points cut, which diminishes or increases the initial width of the piece. This change of width (or tapering) is obtained by all cutting rates or patterns which involve bars or meshes.

As for cuts involving bars, bating or creasing will depend on the choice of one of the two directions parallel to the mesh sides as they appear at the start of the cut. We shall specify how this choice is made in the course of the next operation where the all-bars cutting rate will be described.

By way of illustration, in order to cut obliquely to the direction of the net, rectangular pieces of webbing with a whole number of meshes in width will be used, and each time the cut will be begun on the meshes along the lower edge.

The pieces are usually cut in the direction that tends to diminish the initial width (bating, decreasing); we will do the same in the subsequent operations and finish by a cut in the direction that tends to increase the width (increasing).

3.3.1 Definition of taper ratio

At the beginning of each operation we will indicate the taper ratio: $R = $ Decrease/Depth, corresponding to the cutting rate used.

This taper ratio equals the number of meshes lost in width divided by the number of meshes in depth by the end of which the taper should be achieved (definition adopted by the ISO).

In the cutting calculations, this ratio is multiplied by the depth of the piece of netting to be cut to determine in advance the total bating achieved by the planned cut. Exceptionally the all-bars cut and the mesh-and-bar cut always give a taper equal to the product of the rate by the depth *minus* one mesh. The explanation for this exception is given at the end of the operation that follows.

3.3.2 All-bars cutting technique   Taper ratio: $R = 1/1$

The all-bars cut (Figure 6) is made in the direction parallel to the mesh sides.

Any operation of this type is started on the mesh immediately after the one that delimits the initial width of the piece.

The divergence between the sides of the open corner by one mesh indicates the choice of direction for the cut, all the more clearly the more open the meshes of the piece of netting. Thus the straight line prolongation of one of the sides of the angle gives the direction which tends to diminish initial width; inversely, the prolongation also in a straight line of the other side of this angle will increase this same width.

To put it more precisely, the direction of a cut for diminishing the width (bating) is given by the side of the open angle closest to the mesh that delimits the initial width and the cut for increasing the width (creasing) by the other side of that angle.

To execute this all-bars cut, bating along the right side of a panel one first stretches the netting along the side to the left of the open angle of the mesh to be eliminated; one after another one snips all the mesh sides occurring immediately to the right of the line formed by the prolongation of the left side of the open angle to the level desired, as shown in Figure 6. Then the meshes are cut to separate the piece.

This all-bars cut results, as already mentioned, in a decrease in the initial width equal to the number of meshes in depth *minus* one. This mesh that makes the difference corresponds to the point formed at the beginning of the cut; when the cut is done with creasing, this point is once again found on completion of the operation.

In the last chapter where we explain how wing corners are formed, we will see how the joining of the wing in this case restores the design of the cut and eliminates the point.

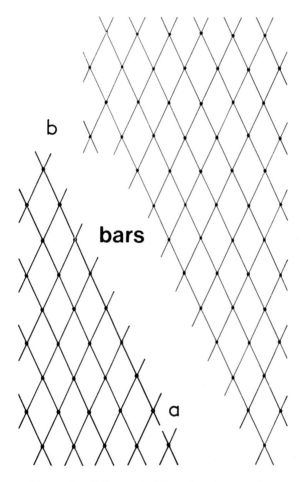

FIGURE 6.—All-bars cut. Triangular piece cut from
a to b started with a point; depth of cut, 4 meshes,
initial decrease in width 4 − 1 = 3 meshes.

3.3.3   POINT-AND-BARS CUTS

These cuts are the result of alternation of one or several points and one or several bars. By way of illustration we will describe how one of these is made on the right edge of a piece cut from a rectangular net.

One point—one bar cutting rate (Figure 7).   *Taper ratio: R = 1/3.*

A start is made on the right-hand portion of the lower edge of the net in order to leave the initial desired width to the left.

In order to bring out the point by which the process is started, one cuts the two sides of the mesh to the right of the intermediary knot after the last

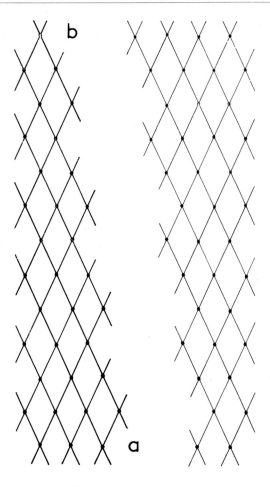

FIGURE 7.—One point, one-bar cutting rate from
a to b.

mesh of the initial width. The bar at which this process finishes is obtained
by cutting the right-hand upper side of the intermediary knot coming after
the point.

This process is repeated continuously, each time forming the point on the
second intermediary knot after the bar (for example: one cuts the two sides
of the mesh to the right of the second intermediary knot coming after the bar,
and so forth).

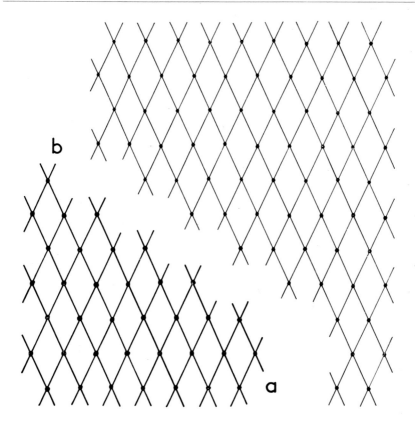

FIGURE 8.—One-point, one-bar cutting rate, from a to b. The cut is started at a point.

3.3.4 MESH-AND-BARS CUTS

These cuts are made by alternating one mesh and one or several successive bars. In this case, the example will involve a cut on the right-hand edge of the piece.

One mesh—one bar cutting rate (Figure 8).

First of all a point is obtained by sectioning the two sides of the mesh to the right of the intermediary knot coming after the last mesh in the initial width of the netting, then the mesh by which the process is begun, by cutting the two sides of the mesh above the intermediary knot that comes after the point; and finally the bar of the process by cutting the upper side of the mesh to the right of the second intermediary knot following the mesh.

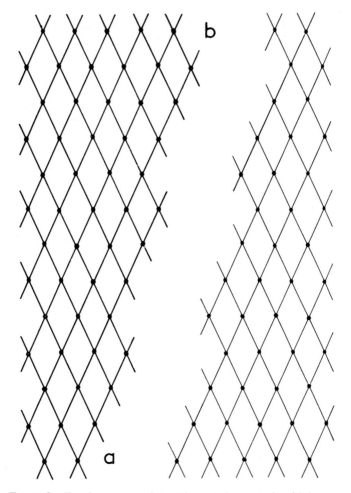

FIGURE 9.—Two bars—one point cutting rate from a to b, with increase.

This process is repeated in continuous fashion starting each time from one bar to obtain the mesh, and not from a point as said above. The mesh by which the process is again started is then formed by eliminating the two sides of the mesh above the intermediary knot following the bar, and so on.

The result of all processes for making this type of cut is marked by the same exception as for the all-bars cut, that is, the presence of a point where the cut starts. As a general rule the cutting of edges with bating always begins with a point.

3.3.5 CUTS WITH CREASING

Panel edges are cut in the direction by which the initial width is increased whenever working conditions do not permit working in the usual direction.

By way of illustration we shall describe how the two bars—one point cut is executed on the right side of the piece to be obtained.

Two bars—one point cutting rate (Figure 9).

Increase ratio: $R = 1/2$.

We shall start on the left side of the lower edge of the panel, after the mesh which sets the initial width on the right-hand side and make the bars by cutting parallel to the prolongation of the right side of the free corner of this mesh:

> The first bar by which the process begins is obtained by cutting the side of the lower right-hand mesh of the intermediary knot following the mesh indicated above;
>
> then, the second bar is made by cutting the lower right-hand mesh side of the intermediary knot that comes after the first bar;
>
> and finally, the point that ends the process by eliminating the two sides of mesh to the right of the intermediary knot following the second bar.

The process is repeated continuously by releasing each time a first bar on the second intermediary knot that comes after the point or, to be more precise, this bar from which the process is repeated is formed by cutting the lower right-hand mesh side of the second intermediary knot that comes after the point, etc.

If the depth of the piece of netting is not an exact multiple of the increased ratio, the final repetition of this process is incomplete. When the cut is with increase, the operation is begun by this shortened process.

CHAPTER 4

4.   **BRAIDING**

The remaking, by mending, of various damaged or torn portions of a net necessarily requires a knowledge of all operations involved in braiding by hand.

Since the special conditions in which mending is done on board ship—limited space, makeshift arrangements, etc.—make it difficult to offer a logical description of the various operations, the description given here is of mending performed in a workshop. Nevertheless, in order to be able to follow closely how work is done on board ship, instead of the spool or net-pin we have used the correct position of the fingers by which the meshes can be measured, as is done in fisheries schools when initiating students in the art of mending.

4.1 Making a rectangular piece of netting

4.1.1 PREPARATIONS FOR THE WORK

For all operations of braiding we will use a headpiece consisting for instance of a rectangular piece of netting with meshes of roughly 40 mm side, 5 to 6 meshes in depth and from 10 to 15 meshes in width with the upper edge meshes passed over the braiding rod. Our materials will include a knife, No. 2 wooden needles and nylon twine of a diameter practically the same as that of the meshes of the headpiece.

4.1.2 SINGLE-TWINE FILLING OF THE NEEDLE

For filling the needle is held in the left hand and the twine is guided by the thumb of the right hand:

> the end of the twine is held momentarily under the thumb at the base of the needle tongue;
> the twine is twisted round the tongue from left to right twice, helped by a slight pressure of the right thumb on the needle just above the tip of the tongue;
> then the thread is caught in the groove at the base of the needle;
> the needle is turned around and the thread is once again guided toward the tongue for a single twist only.

The filling is completed by repeating the last two steps again and again. Later on the method of double-twine filling of the needle will be explained.

4.1.3 MAKING A SINGLE FISHERMAN'S KNOT

Two lengths of about 10 cm of the twines to be joined are placed side by side and then half-knots are made with each of the ends (Figure 10A) catching the other thread. The knot is correctly made if the end of each piece of twine extends out from the completed knot parallel to the general direction of the twine (Figure 10 B).

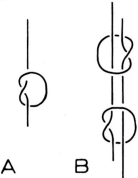

A   B

FIGURE 10.—Single fisherman's knot. A—a half-knot; B—a fisherman's knot.

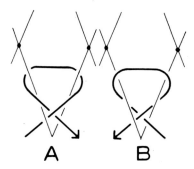

A   B

FIGURE 11.—Single sheet bend. A—knot made when braiding from left to right; B—knot made when braiding from right to left.

4.1.4 MAKING A SINGLE SHEET BEND

As a rule the needle, used for the first time in this operation, will always be held in the right hand.

There are two successive steps:

First step: the needle is introduced from the bottom upward into the first

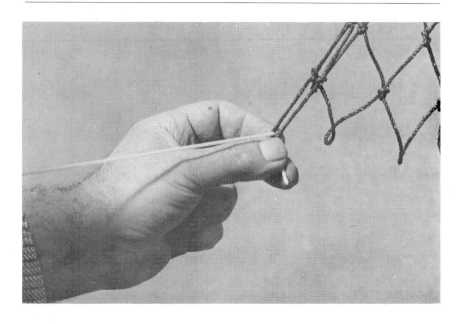

FIGURE 12.—Making the single sheet bend.   A (*above*)—first step; B (*below*)—second step.

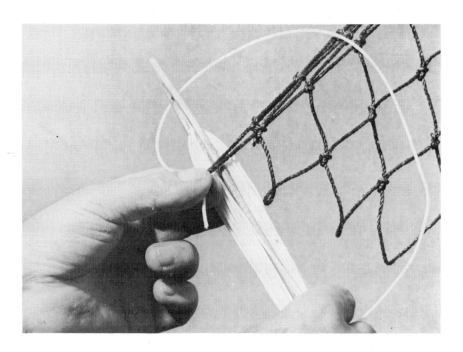

mesh to the left, the free end of the twine being held in the left hand. After drawing the end of the twine out a few centimetres from the mesh by pulling on the needle, this mesh and the twine that goes through it are held tight between the thumb and the index finger (Figure 12A).

Second step: the twine is widely looped above the headpiece, from left to right. With the same movement the needle is passed under the two sides of the mesh so that it appears inside the circle (Figure 12B). The knot is drawn by pulling the needle to oneself (Figure 12C). The sheet bend thus formed in braiding from left to right is shown in Figure 11A. In braiding from right to left, as we shall see later on the knot appears in a different position (Figure 11B).

Whatever the knot to be made on the net, it is always better to pass the needle sideways and not flat in making one or several turns on one or more mesh sides.

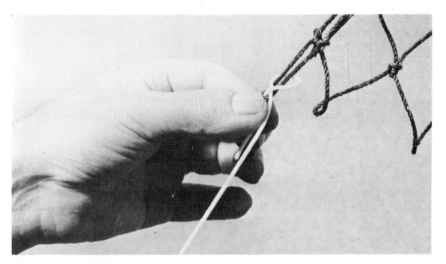

Figure 12 (*continued*).—Making the single sheet bend.   C—drawing the knot by passing the twine under the thumb.

4.1.5   Use of the fingers to measure meshes

In all the braiding and mending operations described by way of illustration in this study, we will make approximately 40 mm meshes. In order to obtain meshes all this size, the ring and third finger of the left hand will be used, placed in different positions depending on whether the first mesh of a row or the following ones have to be measured.

In mending on board ship meshes of all sizes are likely to be used. In this case three or four fingers or even the whole hand are used to measure the largest meshes and only a single finger for the smallest.

In all cases it is necessary in order to reproduce a given meshsize, to gauge the desired size in advance on one mesh of this meshsize.

The way to gauge the size is to insert into the cleaned mesh one or several fingers of the left hand so that, if possible, the base of the sheet bend of the last row braided may be tangential to the upper side of the finger or the several fingers together. If need be, an adjustment is made by pushing one or more of the finger joints into the mesh in order to see the place where the base of the knot comes in relation to the upper part of the one or more fingers used.

In order to carry out this operation properly, the net is pulled slightly in the direction of run of the net by the fingers introduced into the open mesh, the direction being such that the inside and outside faces of each of them touch the twine.

Whatever type of braiding is to be done, the measurement obtained in this way is always the one used for the first mesh of a row and possibly the next ones, whenever the above-described method cannot be employed.

4.1.6 MAKING THE FIRST MESH ON THE LEFT-HAND

After the twine of the needle has been attached to the headpiece by a sheet bend, the first mesh on the left side is braided. This operation can be broken down into three steps

First step: at about 10 cm from the headpiece, on the stretched twine, the ring and third finger of the left hand are placed (with the palm turned downwards) and the twine is held tight between the thumb, below, and the third finger, above, in order to keep the tension exerted on it during the first part of the second step performed by the needle (Figure 13A).

Second step: after the needle has been passed from below into the second mesh to the left, one pulls on the twine, turning the left hand over as required, while allowing it to slip under the ring and third fingers until the desired size of mesh, measured by these two fingers together, is obtained (Figure 13B).

At the end of the second step and in general whenever the twine is pulled during braiding, the stretched twine of the needle is practically parallel to the lower portion of the left arm or else at the smallest possible horizontal angle.

Third step: The twine still being pulled to prevent losing this measurement, the base of the mesh through which it is passed is caught between the tip of the thumb and the index finger; the third finger is then withdrawn from the mesh being made (Figure 13C). By turning the hand toward the left, the sheet bend is completed and drawn tight by passing the thread below and to the right of the left thumb.

These simultaneous movements, pivoting of the left hand and forming the circle during the tying of the sheet bend, renders its execution easier.

The first mesh of the row braided toward the right or toward the left is called the "mother mesh".

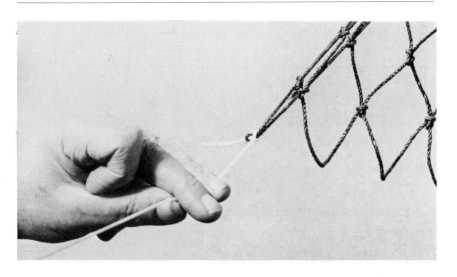

FIGURE 13.—Making the first mesh on the left hand. A (*above*)—first step; B (*below*)—
second step.

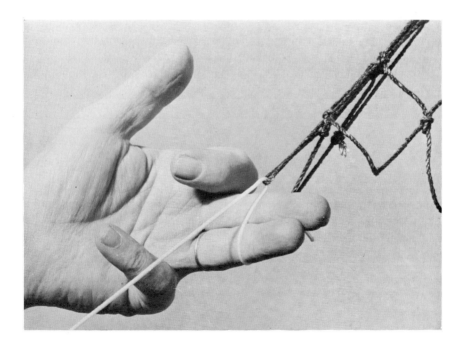

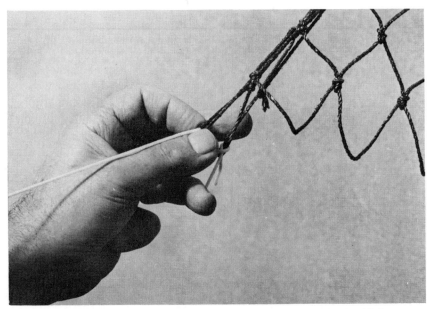

FIGURE 13 (*continued*).—Making the first mesh on the left hand.   C—third step.

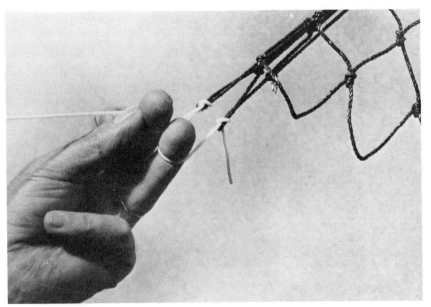

FIGURE 14.—Making the second mesh braiding toward the right.   A—first step.

4.1.7. MAKING THE SECOND MESH AND THE NEXT ONES IN THE SEQUENCE IN BRAIDING TOWARD THE RIGHT

This again will be broken down into three steps.

First step: after having introduced the ring finger of the left hand with the palm turned downward, into the mother mesh, the twine is held between the thumb and the third finger, with the thumb underneath (Figure 14A).

Second step: the needle is passed from the bottom upward through the third mesh of the headpiece; then the thread is pulled until the inside face of the third finger reaches the same level as the ring finger to form a loop of the same size as the preceding mesh (Figure 14B).

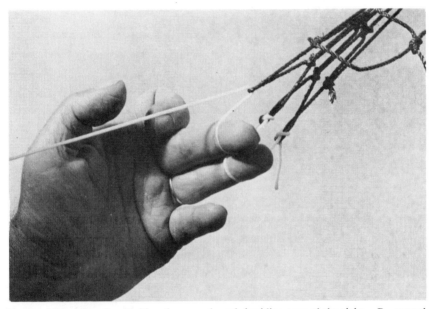

FIGURE 14 (*continued*).—Making the second mesh braiding toward the right.   B—second step.

Third step: one holds the base of the mesh through which the twine is drawn and then the third finger is disengaged from the meshes (Figure 13C); the sheet bend is completed as in the third step of the making of the mother mesh.

The second mesh thus formed is used as the mother mesh for the third; the latter for the fourth and so on until the full desired width is attained.

Still keeping the netting in the same position, braiding can then be continued in the opposite direction, from right to left, by the technique explained in the next paragraph.

When large meshes have to be made it is difficult to displace the thumb and index finger to take hold of the mesh through which the twine is drawn while keeping the ring and third fingers on the same level. In this case in

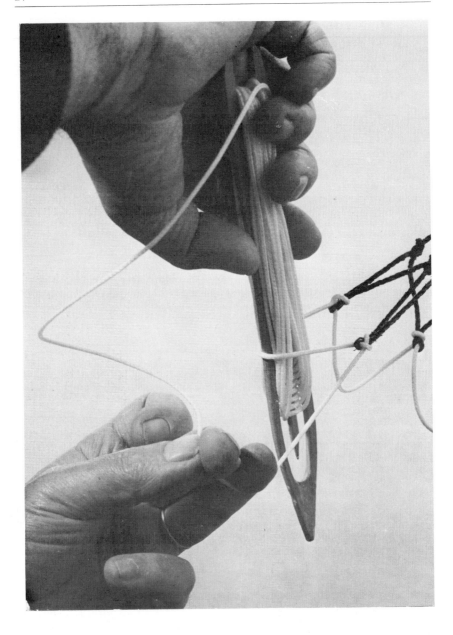

FIGURE 15.—Making the first mesh on the right side. Start of step two.

order to maintain acceptable regularity, each mesh is measured not in relation to the preceding one, but individually as for the first mesh of the row.

4.1.8   MAKING THE FIRST MESH ON THE RIGHT SIDE

Braiding from right to left is not different than from left to right except in the way in which the needle is passed through the open meshes of the preceding row and in the position of the left hand starting from the second mesh.

First step: the taking hold of the twine is the same as for the mesh on the left side (Figure 13A).

Second step: the needle is passed from below upward, to the left and over the left hand into the last mesh braided from left to right (Figure 15). Then one repeats the end of the second step, then the third step by which the first mesh on the left was made (Figure 13B and C).

4.1.9.   MAKING THE SECOND MESH AND THE FOLLOWING ONE IN BRAIDING TOWARD THE LEFT

First step: the ring finger of the left hand is inserted, with the palm turned upward, into the mother mesh and the twine is held between the thumb and the third finger (Figure 16A).

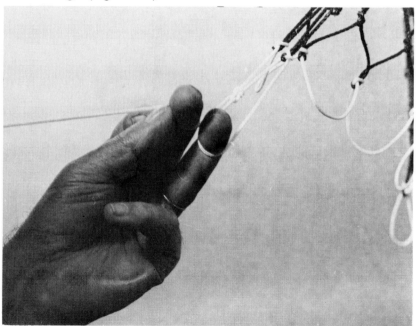

FIGURE 16.—Making the second mesh in braiding toward the left.   A—step one.

FIGURE 16 (*continued*).—Making the second mesh working toward the left.   B—second step.

Second step: the needle is passed from below upward to the left and over the left hand, into the next-to-last mesh braided from left to right (Figure 16B). Then the end of the second step is repeated, then the third step in braiding of the second mesh starting from the left.

The other meshes of the row are made in the same manner as this second mesh, each time taking the preceding mesh as the mother mesh.

After braiding several rows, similar to those described above, a small panel is obtained, the shape of each side edge corresponding to that formed by an all-points cutting rate.

The width of any panel braided by this process is equal at all levels to the number of meshes plus one half-mesh, this is always evident from the bars that appear at the beginning and end of the panel.

4.2 Process of braiding with batings

The shape of the side edges produced by all cutting rates other than all-points is also obtained by braiding of the various components of the cut. Among the various ways of hand braiding the selvedges[1] we have selected the one that entails the minimum risk of deformation of the net due to pulling and which affords the further advantage of reinforcing the edge of the panel without any other artifice.

In the description of braiding by one of the five processes described above, we shall leave out the usual row intended to be cut for separation of the panel from the headpiece. Thus thè first notable feature of this process will appear when the first row or rows are being made in such a way as to shape the side edge, as is normally seen when one panel is attached to another. The details of construction indicated will always refer to the right-hand edge. Obviously by merely turning the panel around the various operations can be performed on the left side in the same manner as on the right. Furthermore, it is always possible to work symmetrically on the left side.

We shall begin by the *all-bars* braiding that will form with the headpiece a design analogous to that with wing corners, often encountered in the join of the wings with the belly or the square.

4.2.1. ALL-BARS BRAIDING PATTERN   Taper ratio: $R = 1/1$

Starting with the first mesh on the left, for instance, continuous braiding is done thus:

making a first row that establishes the initial width of the panel;

---

[1] The phrase "various ways of braiding the selvedges" covers:
   braiding with meshes pinched together on three twines;
   braiding without pinching any mesh but where only the bars for bating or increasing are doubled;
   braiding without a pinched mesh but where increasing and bating are done inside the net close to the selvedge which then consists of points only.

then, a second row, the first mesh of which is completed by a sheet bend on three pieces of twine, that is the two pieces of the supporting mesh plus the twine of the mesh being made, which therefore is pinched in the middle (Figure 17A).

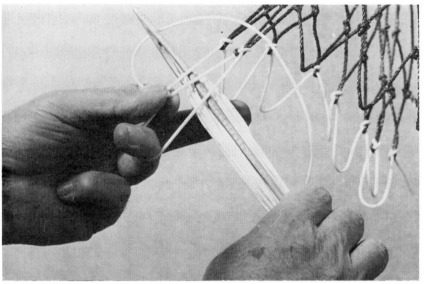

FIGURE 17.—Braiding with batings.   A—making a pinched mesh.

In this manner the point on the right-hand edge is eliminated with the result that two bars are formed in the present construction, one on the preceding row and the other at the level of the three-twine knot, as well as a close loop extending the second bar. This loop, which professionals call "bating" is of the same depth as the mother-mesh that it replaces and, like it, serves to give the measurement for the next mesh.

From now one we shall use the abbreviated term *pinched mesh* for any point gripped or pinched in the centre by the sheet bend on three pieces of twine (Figure 18).

After the second row, one braids:

> a third row, the terminal mesh of which is formed by taking *together*, as a support, the last mesh and loop of the preceding row (Figure 17B);
> a fourth row including a first pinched mesh.

These last two rows are then repeated again and again, continuously.

This construction gives on the right edge a series of mesh sides alternately in double twine and triple twine which effectively reinforces the selvedge (Figure 18B).

It should be stipulated that the pinched mesh does not necessarily form two bars, as will be shown further on. On the other hand it always produces a loop which, taken by itself or together with a nearby open mesh, becomes a support for the last mesh of the next row.

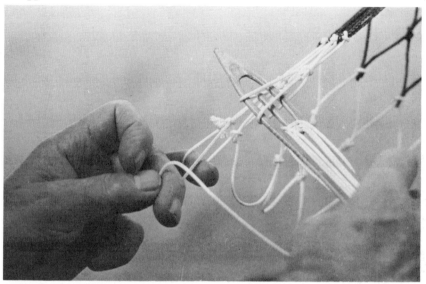

FIGURE 17 (*continued*).—Braiding with batings. B—ending of a row on the mesh and loop.

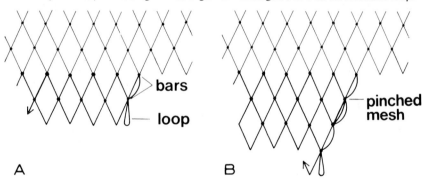

FIGURE 18.—All-bars braiding pattern. A—first pinched point; B—all-bars reinforced selvedge in braiding with batings.

4.2.2. ONE POINT—TWO BARS BRAIDING   Taper ratio: $R = 1/2$

Starting with the mesh on the left, the process goes forward by continuous construction as follows:

> one complete row from left to right;
> a second row, the first mesh of which becomes the point of the process on the right hand edge (Figure 19A);
> a third complete row;

a fourth complete row, the first mesh of which is pinched to form two bars, as mentioned above.

Once the fourth row has been braided, the following process is repeated continuously. One braids:

a fifth row, the terminal mesh of which is made by taking together, as a support, the last mesh and loop of the preceding row;
a sixth row, the first mesh of which provides the point on the right edge (Figure 19B);
a complete seventh row;
an eighth row, the first mesh of which is pinched in order to obtain two bars.

The points made by this braiding process are all single twine; the same holds for those involving an even number of bars. Nevertheless, if accidentally one begins the braiding by shifting the pinched mesh by one row, for instance during mending, all points are in double twine; the way in which this is done is described in the following operation.

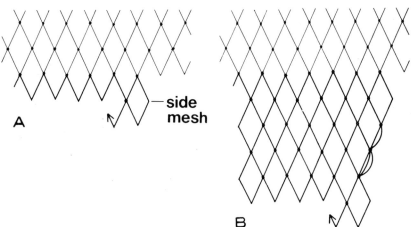

FIGURE 19.—One point—two bars braiding pattern. A—point in single twine of this process; B—start of repetition of this process.

4.2.3. ONE POINT—ONE BAR BRAIDING Taper ratio: $R = 1/3$

Starting with the first mesh on the left, the process consists of the following continuous construction:

making an initial complete row from left to right;
a second row, the first mesh of which constitutes the point of the process on the right edge;
a third row, the terminal mesh of which forms the bar of the process (Figure 20A).

Three rows are enough to repeat the process but the order set for renewing the same details of construction is reached between the second and seventh rows. Then the braiding continues, thus:

a fourth row including an initial pinched mesh;
a fifth row, the first two meshes of which are braided on the last mesh and loop of the preceding row, taken separately for support;
a sixth row including a first pinched mesh (Figure 20B) (this phase of the operation completes the making of the doubled point);
a seventh row, the terminal mesh of which is made by taking together, as a support, the last open mesh and loop of the preceding row.

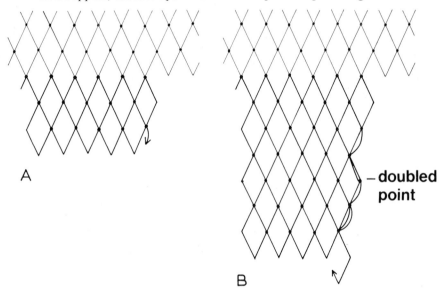

**– doubled
point**

A

B

FIGURE 20.—One point—one bar braiding process. A—end of the process; B—pinched mesh terminating the doubled point.

The points obtained by this braiding process are alternately in single twine then in double twine; the same is true when the process involves an uneven numbers of bars. Whatever the latter may be, the point in double twine is always made as just described.

If by mistake one forgets the pinched mesh that terminates the point in double twine, the width is increased by a half-mesh at this level, which is shown by an increase of one bar located before the point; this point is then made of a single twine and shifted by one row.

In this connection we stipulate that, on the oblique side of a panel, two sides of mesh linked by any bar whatsoever always lie in the same oblique direction; when these two sides are aligned in an opposite direction, some mistake must have occurred in the braiding or the cutting of the selvedge.

The description we have just given of these three braiding techniques

shows all details of construction necessary during the braiding operations
of one selvedge with bating in width and involving points and bars.

In the two following operations we shall describe the process of braiding
in *bars and mesh* generally used to make the inner edges of the wings of
pelagic trawls. The precautions to be taken to begin braiding of these
selvedges are indicated in Chapter D dealing with the making and mounting
of sections.

We shall take as an example one portion of the process of two bars—
one mesh braiding to illustrate how selvedges are constructed with mesh
and even number of bars as well as the process of one bar—one mesh braiding
for selvedges with mesh and uneven number of bars.

4.2.4. TWO BARS—ONE MESH BRAIDING PROCESS   Taper ratio: $R = 2/1$

Starting from any mesh whatsoever on the right side of the heading,
continuous braiding is done as follows:

> a first row from right to left, the first sheet bend made on any mesh of
> the headpiece whatsoever forming with it a bar by which the process
> begins;
> a second row, the final sheet bend of which, being made on the last
> mesh of the preceding row, forms the second bar; the last mesh is
> then doubled by braiding in the opposite direction along the same
> row (Figure 21A).

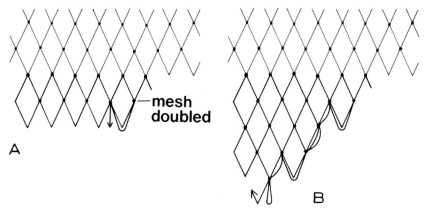

FIGURE 21.—Braiding to two bars—one mesh process. A—mesh doubled by braiding in
the opposite direction; B—braiding of two bars—one mesh selvedge.

This second row completes the process. Continuous forming of the
selvedge is done by braiding a third and fourth row and then repeating. In
this way one obtains:

> a third row containing one first pinched mesh;
> a fourth row, the terminal mesh of which is first braided by taking

together as a support, the last mesh and loop of the preceding row, then is doubled like that of the second row (Figure 21B);
a fifth row like the third;
a sixth row like the fourth, and so on.

The meshes braided in this manner are all in double twine. The same holds true for all bars and mesh braiding processes involving an even number of bars. Nevertheless if one accidently begins the work by shifting the pinched mesh by one row, all the meshes are formed of a single twine together with a loop. In the following operation we shall see how one of these meshes is made.

4.2.5   ONE BAR—ONE MESH BRAIDING   Taper ratio: $R = 3/1$

Starting from any mesh whatsoever, on the right-hand side of the head-piece, continuous braiding is done as follows:

a first row from right to left is enough for the process. As a matter of fact a bar is formed at the beginning by braiding on the mesh of the headpiece and the mesh for the process is obtained by making the first mesh of the row.

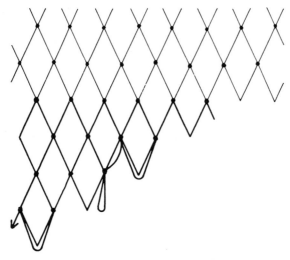

FIGURE 22.—One bar—one mesh braiding process.

One row is enough to start the process but the order imposed by repetition of the same details of construction is determined by the second and third rows; braiding goes as follows:

a second row with one mesh less to leave on the right a mesh in the preceding row;

the last mesh is then doubled by braiding in the opposite direction;
a third row, including an initial pinched mesh (Figure 22);
a fourth row like the second;
a fifth row like the third and so on.

The meshes made in this way are alternately in single twine with a loop
and then in double twine. The same happens in all the bars and mesh braiding
processes with an uneven number of bars.

The mesh and loop that are made at the same time are connected during
the mounting on the leadlines.

4.3   Braiding process with increase

In the workshop as a rule oblique selvedges are generally made with
bating. However those that raise no particular problem for execution with
increase, such as all-bars or point-and-bars selvedges are braided in either
direction indifferently. During the next three operations we shall describe,
by way of illustration, three processes of braiding with increase chosen from
among those performed in workshops. Each of them begins after braiding
of a first row that is to be cut to separate the panel from the headpiece and
the details of construction given will always refer to the right edge.

4.3.1   ALL-BARS BRAIDING   Increase ratio: $R = 1/1$

Starting out from any mesh whatsoever, in the middle of the headpiece
for instance, continuous braiding is done as follows:

a first row from right to left;
a second row at the end of which an extra loop is formed (Figure 23A)
measuring it as though it were a mesh and connecting it with the
last mesh of the preceding row;

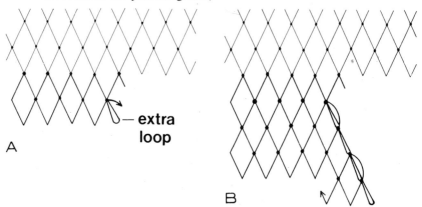

FIGURE 23.—All-bars braiding process with increase.   A—extra loop braided at the end
of the second row; B—all-bars selvedge with increase.

a third row including a first pinched mesh obtained by taking the loop of the preceding row as a support;
a fourth row like the second;
a fifth row like the third (Figure 23B), etc.

We stipulate that in braiding with increase, the extra loop, that is made only in this case, as well as the one formed by the pinched mesh are always taken separately as a support for either a mesh or another loop.

4.3.2 TWO BARS—ONE POINT BRAIDING   Increase ratio: $R = 1/2$

Starting from any mesh whatsoever of the central portion of the head-piece, continuous braiding is done as follows:

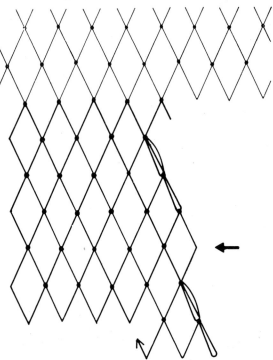

FIGURE 24.—Two bars—one point braiding with increase. The arrow marks the end of the process with the single twine point.

a first row from right to left, after which the actual braiding starts;
a second row ending in an extra loop;
a third row involving a first mesh pinched on the above loop;
a fourth row, the last mesh of which is braided on the loop of the pinched mesh;

a fifth row, the first mesh of which forms the point which completes
the process (Figure 24).

Braiding is continued by repeating the process each time from the second
to the fifth rows.

4.3.3   ONE BAR—ONE POINT BRAIDING   Increase ratio: $R = 1/3$

Starting with any mesh in the middle of the headpiece, continuous
braiding is done thus:

> a first row from right to left, after which the process begins;
> a second row ending in an extra loop;
> a third row including the first mesh pinched on the loop;
> a fourth row, the last mesh of which is braided on the loop of the
> pinched mesh, completing the process (Figure 25A).

Three rows suffice to get this process started but the order imposed for
repetition of the same details of construction is obtained on six rows. Thus
the braiding continues as follows:

> one fifth row, which involves a first pinched mesh;
> a sixth row, the last mesh of which is braided on the loop of the
> pinched mesh;
> a seventh row, beginning with a point (Figure 25B).

Braiding continues by repeating the process starting from the second row.

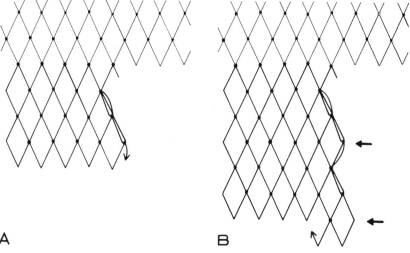

A   B

FIGURE 25.—Process of one bar—one point braiding with increase.   A—end of process;
B—alternation of single twine and double twine points.

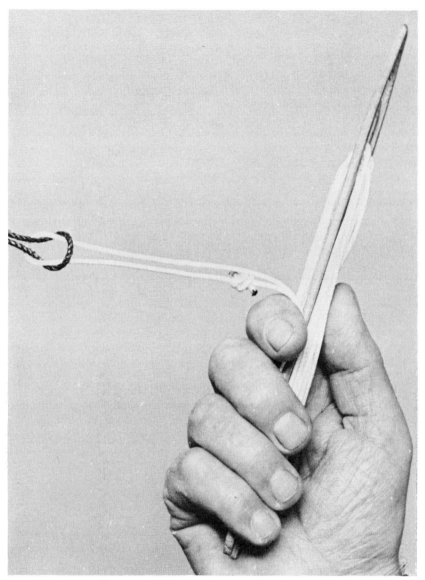

FIGURE 26.—Tying up two needlefuls.

4.4 Process of braiding of flymeshes on wings

We shall complete the braiding operations by the fashioning of flymeshes usually located on the inner edges of the wings of bottom trawls.

4

These flymeshes that the fishermen also call hanging meshes are usually braided either starting from a one point-one mesh cut or else from a one point-two meshes cut. They are obtained by braiding reinforcements that border the wings or directly on one or another of these cuts previously made on the wing during repairing of the net on board ship, for instance. The last procedure is described in the chapter on "Net Mending".

A flymesh is about one and a half times the size of the mesh on which it is built. When wing meshes are already of considerable size it is impossible to measure the largest ones without the help of a spool. When nets are mended on board ship without a spool, they are formed by sight comparison with those that were not broken.

During the next operations we shall describe, on the one hand, how the needle is filled with double twine for use in braiding of flymeshes and, on the other, how the latter are formed with bating as is usual in workshops.

The making of these flymeshes with increase, in the direction selected on board ship when best suited to working conditions, is described at the end of the chapter on Net Mending.

4.4.1   FILLING THE NEEDLE WITH DOUBLE TWINE

In order to fill a needle with a double twine, the length of twine necessary is unwound, about 10 m for a No. 2 wooden needle; the middle portion of this length is then placed on the tongue the ends being from 15 to 20 cm different in length; then the filling is done by guiding the double twine as if it were single.

Once the needle has been filled, one ties the two uneven length ends together with a simple fisherman's knot. This manner of completing the filling, by a loop and a knot at some distance from the ends tying the two single pieces of twine, has the advantage on the one hand of making it possible by braiding the loops (Figure 26) to quickly tie up the ends of two needlefuls while avoiding accumulation of many large knots during the process.

4.4.2   BRAIDING OF FLYMESHES (FIGURE 27)   Taper ratio: $R = 1/1$

We will begin this operation and the next without mentioning the row normally intended to be destroyed when the headpiece and the panel are separated.

Starting on the first free mesh of the headpiece, at the left, continuous braiding is done as follows:

a first row corresponding to the initial width of the panel;
a second row, the first mesh of which is one and a half times longer than the normal mesh;
a third row that leaves the flymesh mentioned above free;
a fourth row like the second;
a fifth row like the third, etc.

Every two rows one obtains a flymesh left free. Since this mesh is supported on the last free mesh of the preceding row, there is a decrease in width of one mesh in two rows.

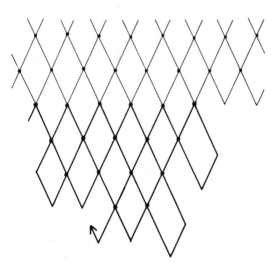

FIGURE 27.—Process of braiding flymeshes ($R = 1/1$).

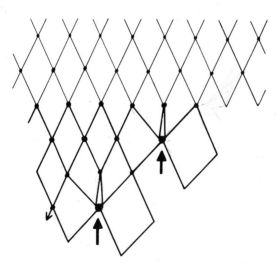

FIGURE 28.—Process of braiding flymeshes ($R = 2/1$).
The arrows mark the knots tying together the last two
meshes of the preceding row.

4.4.3   BRAIDING OF FLYMESHES (FIGURE 28)   Taper ratio: $R = 2/1$

Starting on the first mesh of the headpiece, on the left, continuous braiding is done as follows:

> an initial row;
> a second row, the first mesh of which is as long as the flymeshes of the preceding operation, formed by using as a support the last two meshes braided;
> a third row that leaves the flymesh free;
> a fourth row like the second;
> a fifth row like the third, etc.

Since the flymesh is based on the last two meshes braided in the preceding row, the decrease in this case is two meshes in two rows.

CHAPTER 5

5.   NET MENDING

The last two chapters were devoted to essential know-how for mending proper, that is to say repairing of nets. This chapter will be begun by a description of two operations that precede mending. Then we will describe the way in which various repairs are made—from mending a simple tear to the replacement of a net section.

5.1   Work preliminary to mending a tear

The operation of preparing the edges of a tear before repairing it is called by professionals "trimming" or "clean cutting".

5.1.1   TRIMMING A TEAR

The edges of a tear are cleaned up in order to eliminate bars not needed for the mending, and which actually hamper the continuous remaking of missing meshes. When this operation is correctly performed the edges consist of only points and meshes plus two bars, one for the start of the repair and the other to finish it.

The trimming and subsequent mending are done in the direction of the netting and moving backwards. In this way when the torn piece is placed on the trestle hooks so that the netting direction is the same as for braiding the general direction of the work is from top to bottom of the tear. Accordingly, the starting bar will be in the upper portion and the end bar in the lower portion.

Very often the starting bar is already in the row above or the one immediately below it. If not, one side of a mesh at the base of an intermediary knot is cut in the upper part of the tear. After this bar, the trimming is done along one of the edges of the tear, checking the knots one after the other in order to keep only those connecting two or four mesh sides. On coming across a bar one cuts one of the sides in order to obtain a mesh or a point. Once the lower part of the cut is reached, one goes back to the starting bar and repeats the operation on the other edge. By the end of this operation, the terminal bar is at the lowest level (Figure 29).

In trimming the greatest attention has to be paid not to commit the error of leaving a bar on one of the edges, which would make it necessary to resume the work from that point. In the case of a large tear, where trimming is done in sequential sections as the mending progresses, it is possible to make up for a missed bar by leaving another bar at the same level on the other edge; actually in tears on the inside of a net, the bars always have to be in even numbers.

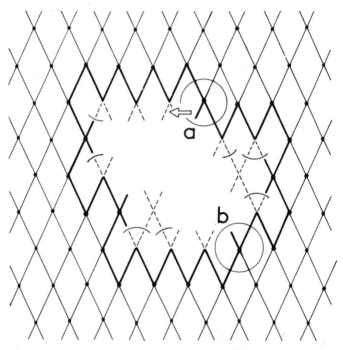

FIGURE 29.—Trimming a tear. a—starting bar and direction of the start of mending; b—terminal bar. The broken lines indicate the sides of meshes eliminated during trimming.

In this case mending is not continuous. The two extra bars are used one to finish the first part of the job and the other as the point of departure to complete the repair of the net.

5.1.2 ELIMINATION OF KNOTS ON MESHES

Starting with a panel mounted on the braiding rod as indicated above, all the knots of a row are of the same design as those of the following row, by turning round, if the panel was braided by hand, or by turning it upside down if the panel was machine-made. Whatever the method of construction, the knot connecting one mesh to another always looks like a single sheet bend formed on a loop.

Thus the twine to be cut in order to undo the knot on a mesh will be either the sheet bend itself or the twine of the loop on which it is formed.

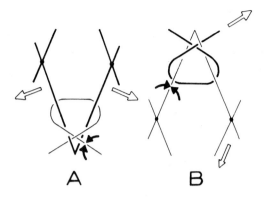

FIGURE 30.—Elimination of knots on meshes. A—
elimination of the sheet bend; B—elimination of the
loop. The black arrows indicate the thread to be cut,
the white arrows the direction of pull.

In the first instance, one first clips as far as the knot the free end of the
twine that does not go through the loop; then one pulls in the opposite
direction on two sides of the mesh to be disengaged in order to open the knot
and release the cut twine (Figure 30A).

In the second case, one of the two free ends of the twine issuing from
the sheet bend is cut even with the knot. Then one pulls in the opposite
direction, on the one hand, and on the side of the free angle of the mesh
going through the loop to be removed, on the other hand (Figure 30B).

This way of eliminating knots on the meshes involves the least risk of
wound with the knife. It is practically the only one used on fine twine panels
as well as the one most commonly used in workshops on new panels made
of heavier twine. When the knots are very tight, as happens with worn out
trawl net sections, very often better results are obtained by directly cutting
the right piece of twine on the knot itself and not around it as indicated
above.

5.2   Repairs of tears on the inside of a panel

In order to repair tears, needles filled with either single or double twine
will be used depending on the kind of pieces to be mended. The net pieces
to be mended will be hung on the trestle hooks or braiding rod presenting
the direction of the netting as indicated in the preceding operations.

We shall start by the description of a few simple examples of mending in
which we will indicate how the three following knots are made: (1) double
sheet bend on starting and finishing bars; (2) single sheet bend on so-called
"pick-up" meshes, the free angle of which appears in a direction opposite
to that of the meshes made in manual braiding; (3) side knot on the point.

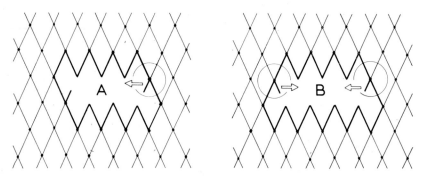

FIGURE 31.—Horizontal tear.   A—the two bars are not at the same level: the start is made on the upper bar; the arrow shows the direction of mending; B—the two bars are at the same level: the start is made either on the left or the right, indifferently.

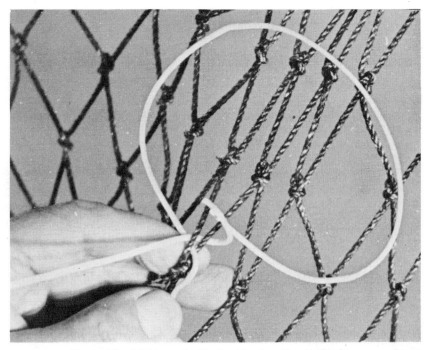

FIGURE 32.—Making a double sheet bend on the starting bar.

5.2.1   REPAIR OF THE SIMPLEST TEAR

A side of a mesh cut on the inside of a piece of netting represents the simplest tear, with only the two bars necessary for mending. For mending the first step is to tie the thread in the needle with a double sheet bend to the uppermost bar; then the gap is filled in by the same kind of knot on the

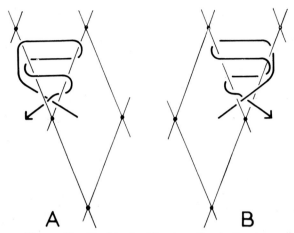

FIGURE 33.—Double sheet bend on the starting bar.
A—knot made in mending going toward the left;
B—knot made in mending going toward the right.

end bar, leaving between these two points of attachment a length of twine
equal to one mesh side.

The way to make a double sheet bend, first on the starting bar and then
on the end bar will be described in the next operation.

Mending of a tear is started by going either toward the left or toward the
right. The way the needle is introduced either into the mesh on which the
double sheet bend is made at the start of the operation or else into the meshes
during mending will depend, as in braiding, on the direction in which the
work is being done. By operating in this manner the thread always comes
out of the knot in the direction of the mending, thus avoiding the formation
of a half-turn on the mesh sides at this spot.

5.2.2   REPAIR OF A HORIZONTAL TEAR

The description of how such a tear is mended is intended essentially to
explain how double sheet bends are made on the starting and finishing bars
and how a single sheet bend is made on the meshes to be picked up.

We shall assume that only a single row inside the panel was torn and that
it has, after trimming, only a few meshes and the starting and finishing bars
respectively to the right at the upper level and to the left at the lower level
(Figure 31A).

We shall break down this mending into four steps.

First step: double sheet bend on the starting bar (Figure 32).

First of all the netting is pulled taut by a finger inserted into one of the
lower meshes, after the bar.

Since braiding is to be done toward the left, the needle is then put from
above through the mesh, the lower sides of which end in the bar, the end of
the twine being held in the left hand.

FIGURE 34.—Single sheet bend on the mesh to be picked up.　A (*above*)—correct position of the mesh; B (*below*)—passing the needle through.

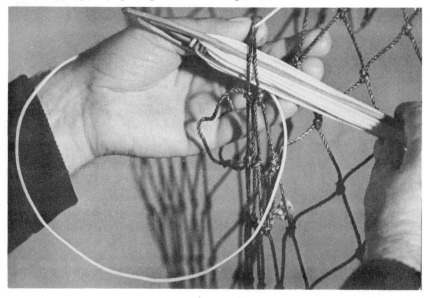

　　Then the knot is made like the single sheet bend but with a double turn, instead of a single one, on the two mesh sides (Figure 33 A and B).

　　Second step: single sheet bend on the mesh to be picked up.

　　The free angle of the first mesh to be picked up is held open between the thumb and the index finger so that the needle is passed through in the direction of the trestle.

FIGURE 34 (*continued*).—Single sheet bend on the mesh to be picked up.   C—tightening the knot. Note how the thumb is released.

By moving the needle toward the left shoulder, the twine is tightened in order to slip the mesh up to the point that the summit of the angle is at the same level as that of the mesh beside it on the same row (Figure 34A).

The twine is held tight at this level between the thumb and the index finger and then, the hand being open with the palm turned upward, the single sheet bend is made on the mesh by describing this time a large circle with the thread on the lower arm in a counter-clockwise direction (Figure 34B).

The knot is tightened by drawing on the thread in the direction of the rod, while pulling in the opposite direction, either with one finger inserted into the mesh itself or into the one below it or else by holding both sides of the latter if the meshes are too large for this. In order to be able to disengage the thumb to tighten the knot the mesh and the twine going through it are held tight between the index finger and the third finger in order not to lose the measurement of the mesh side (Figure 34C).

Third step: continuous mending.

Once the knot has been made on the pick-up mesh, a sheet bend is made on the mesh located immediately to the left of the starting bar, after the last knot formed has been set back at the level of those of same row. Then the mending is continued by connecting the meshes of the upper row to the pick-up meshes one after another.

Fourth step: double sheet bend on end bar (Figure 35).

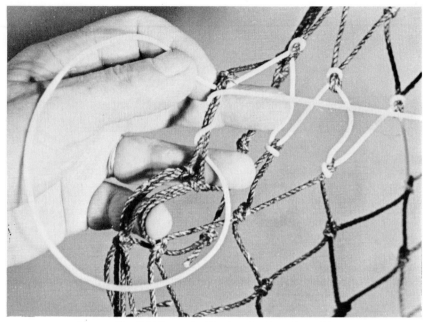

FIGURE 35.—Making a double sheet-bend on the end bar.

The needle is passed, from below upwards, through the mesh the two upper sides of which end at the lower portion of the bar, as for a pick-up mesh, but a double sheet bend instead of a single one is made.

5.2.3 MENDING OF A VERTICAL TEAR

This example is chosen in order to describe how a side knot is made.

It will be assumed that this tear comprises all points on the inside of the panel, without cutting into the edges with meshes, and that the bar formed at each end is located on the left side of the tear (Figure 36).

The mending will be broken down into three steps.

First step: side knot on the right (Figure 37).

After the twine in the needle is attached to the starting bar by a double sheet bend, this time going through the mesh from below upwards, a right-hand side knot is made as follows:

> the right side of the tear is held taut with the ring finger or the little finger put into a mesh in such a way as to bring the knot of the first side mesh onto the tip of the index finger;
>
> the taut thread is placed on the bottom and to the left of the above knot and then held under the thumb, the length being equal to one mesh side;
>
> The needle is put into the side mesh opened by the third finger and

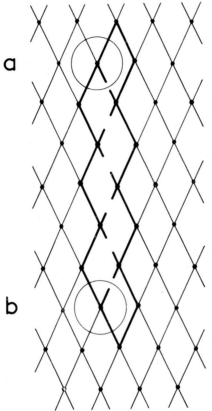

FIGURE 36.—Vertical tear. (a) starting bar and (b) end bar.

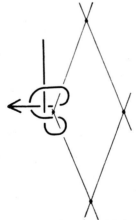

FIGURE 37.—Side knot toward the right.

FIGURE 38.—Making the side knot on the right. A—making the first half hitch.

pulled out between it and the pinched thread to form a half hitch at the base of the knot (Figure 38A);

the half hitch is taken between the thumb and the index finger in order to make a second half hitch on the two threads to be connected— that of the side mesh and that of the mesh being made (Figure 38B).

Second step: side knot on the left.

The knot on the first point on the left is made in the same way as above (Figure 39A), but the third step starts as follows:

the left hand is turned until the palm faces toward oneself; the needle is then put into the point opened by the third finger, etc. (Figure 39B).

Third step: continuous mending and end of repair.

The mending is continued by repeating the first and second steps one after another on the right-hand and left-hand sides meshes until one reaches the last point on the right-hand side. Finally it is completed by connecting the latter to the end bar, as in the fourth step of the preceding operation.

5.2.4   MENDING A RECTANGULAR TEAR

The description of the way that such a tear and the one in the next paragraph are mended will enable us to analyse mending of a single tear in the inside of the net.

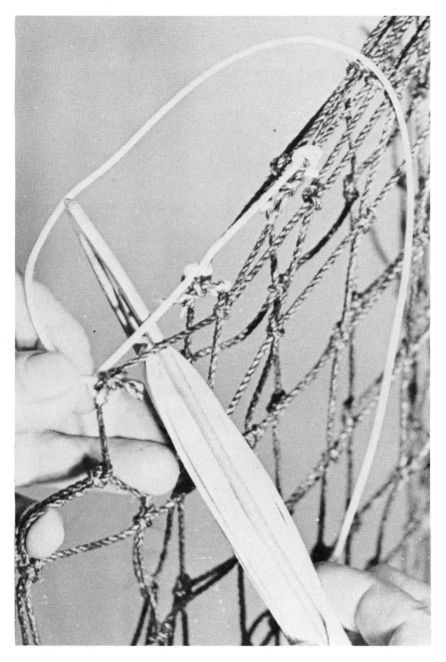

FIGURE 38 (*continued*).—Making the side knot on the right. B—making the second half-hitch.

FIGURE 39.—Making the side knot on the left. A (*above*)—making the first half hitch. Note that the thread is again placed to the left of the knot of the side mesh; B (*below*)—making the second half hitch.

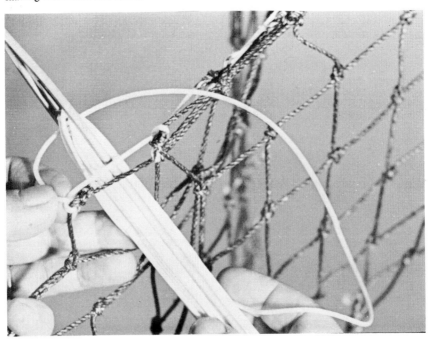

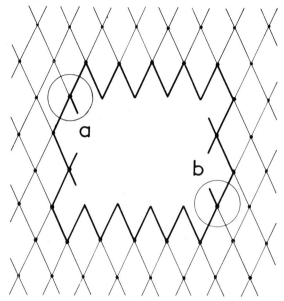

FIGURE 40.—Rectangular tear. a—starting bar; b—end bar.

First of all we will describe the mending of a rectangular breach the depth and width of which are equal to that of several whole meshes plus a half-mesh. This breach will then have two sides made of meshes, two sides with points and two diagonally opposite bars (Figure 40).

Mending such a tear is done as follows:

After the double sheet bend is made on the starting bar, for instance one located on the left, braiding is done on the meshes up to the right side edge where the first point is fixed. Then braiding is done toward the left, until one reaches the point; braiding is repeated alternately first in one direction and then in the other until the last point not followed by a bar is reached. From that mesh on, the breach is closed as indicated for a horizontal tear, picking up in succession the meshes of the lower edge and ending on the finishing bar with a double sheet bend.

Particular case of the so-called "knotless" netting. Mending in this type of panel is done in exactly the same manner as explained in this paragraph and the ones following it; however it will have two special features:

During trimming, it is best to leave at each mesh intersection around the tear, fragments of the mesh sides at least 1 cm long; because of certain manufacturing processes, it seems necessary however to reinforce the contour of the tear either during mending or else, more easily, afterwards in order to provide a support for the mending twine in case the netting twine slips.

A drawing, top left p. 54, shows repair of a tear in a knotless netting:

5

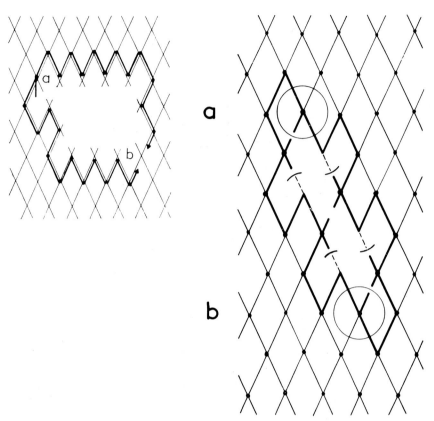

FIGURE 41.—Trimmed oblique tear. a and b—
starting and end bars.

the reinforcement is laced in two steps all around the tear (a-starting point
for the reinforcement lacing in each direction; b-finishing point of lacing),
showing the fragments of mesh sides left after trimming (to facilitate under-
standing of the drawing, the mending is not shown).

5.2.5 MENDING AN OBLIQUE TEAR

We shall explain how to mend a tear, in this case in the inside of the
panel, parallel to the mesh sides and in a single direction, for example
toward the right starting from the upper portion. After trimming, the tear
will have the starting and end bars and an alternating point and mesh on
each edge (Figure 41).

Having made the double sheet on the starting bar, located here on the
right side of the tear, the first point on the left side is attached and then,
mending toward the right, one after another the pick-up mesh, the mesh
on the row above, and the first point on the right-hand side.

FIGURE 42.—Working upward case.   a—starting bar;
b—mending upward; c—end bar.

Then these steps are repeated until one reaches the end bar on which one
ties a double sheet bend.

Generally speaking during the mending of a tear that does not involve
the edge of a panel, the mending process calls for the following remarks:

> from the start on the bar, one reaches the opposite side by picking
> up all the meshes one comes across;
> changing the direction of the work, from leftward to rightward and
> vice versa, is always done at the point of junction of a point.
> Immmediately afterwards, where necessary, one joins up the one or
> several meshes to be picked up except in the case where the last
> point comes just before the end bar or else a bar skipped by mistake,
> or yet another point.

5.2.6   MENDING GOING UPWARD

It is frequently necessary even in small tears to mend by going upward
one or several meshes during the repair. This particular case in mending can
be explained by starting from a horizontal tear involving one mesh cut on
the upper portion. This additional break will be trimmed to form two points
separated by another mesh (Figure 42).

The repair of the tear is done from the right to the left, as the example
shows, up to the point where working back toward the extra gap becomes

FIGURE 43.—Mending upward.   A—position of the fingers on the point.

necessary to furnish the support lacking to the last mesh picked up. Starting from the latter, a half-knot is made on the twine at a distance equal to one mesh side to mark the side mesh, which is accomplished as follows:

> the panel is held taut by the ring finger or the little finger, introduced into one of the meshes, so that the knot of the point of the right side of the gap is placed on the tip of the index finger;
>
> a halfhitch is made on the point and just above the knot, the twine being pushed aside with the thumb to make it easier (Figure 43A);
>
> the size of the mesh being made is adjusted by pulling on the twine and keeping the halfhitch on the index finger in order to make a second halfhitch that will fix the two sides of the mesh to be joined together at the base of the knot of the point (Figure 43B). This second half-hitch is made in the same way as the sheet bend is made on a pick-up mesh; thus the large circle is described on the forearm in a counter-clockwise direction; this knot can be made more easily by pushing the twine aside with the thumb.

The mending is continued by connecting up one after another: going toward the left, the mesh and the point; going toward the right, the point that has just been made by going upward (Figure 43C), then from this point where the tear once again consists entirely of meshes, mending is done toward the left in order to terminate on the end bar.

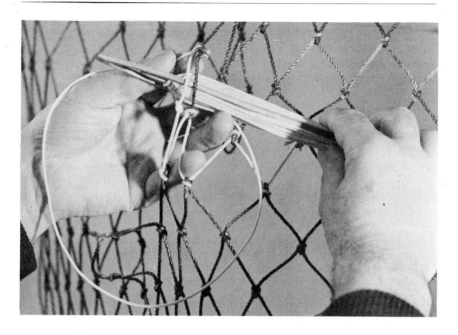

FIGURE 43 (*continued*).—Mending upward. B (*above*)—making a knot on the point; C (*below*)—the mending completed.

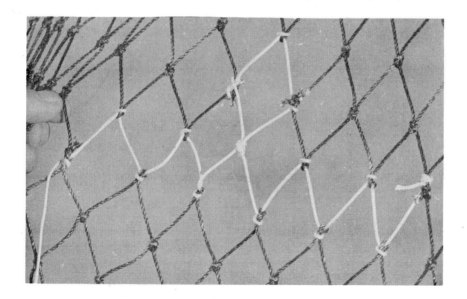

5.2.7   MENDING OF A TEAR IN TWO STEPS

When a tear necessitates working upward on more than two or three meshes, it is repaired by mending the small tear in the normal direction before mending the main tear.

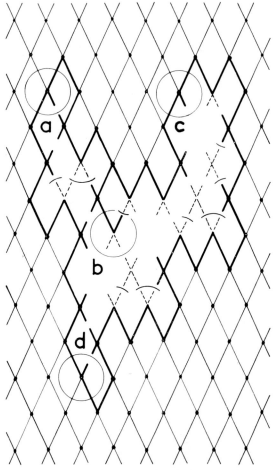

FIGURE 44.—Complex tear necessitating mending in two steps. First step: a—starting bar; b—finishing point. This mesh will become the point after the second part of the tear has been trimmed. Second step: c and d—starting and finishing bars.

The procedure is as follows:

First step: the smallest tear is trimmed like any ordinary tear but the work is stopped at the point where the damage direction is upward. This first part of the tear is mended to the point where working toward the other side is no longer possible because of the lack of the point needed to return to the other side (Figure 44);

Second step: the trimming and then the mending of the main tear is now done as for a simple tear.

On board ship, when the tear is very large and spread in several directions, mending is done simultaneously by two or more menders working toward one another.

5.2.8   INSERTING A PATCH IN THE INSIDE OF A PANEL

When the tear needs too much braiding to sew up the sides, the repair is done by replacing the damaged portion of the net by a patch of netting of the same meshsize. In order to avoid complicating the work, the hole prepared is generally square or rectangular in shape, without any bars, like the patch itself. However, when bars are left in the hole, the patch has to have the same number, and at the same places, so they can be connected in the course of the work.

It is to be remembered that a hole or a patch without bars involves a whole number of meshes in height and in width. When one of these dimensions equals a whole number of meshes plus one half-mesh, the hole or the patch has two bars at places corresponding to the said dimension.

Thus in case there are a fractional number of meshes:

in height, there is one bar at each extremity of one side in meshes (Figure 45A);
in width, there is one bar at each end of one side in points (Figure 45B);
in both height and width, the bars are diagonally opposite each other (Figure 45C).

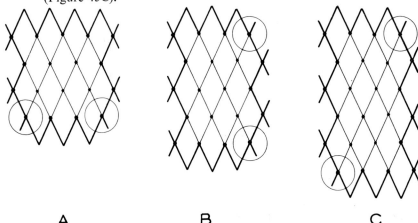

A   **B**   **C**

FIGURE 45.—Position of the bars in a rectangular patch.   A—fractional height; B—fractional width; C—fractional height and width.

The insertion of a patch without bars on the inside of a net, the execution of which we will describe, has as an advantage, first, that it eliminates superposition of knots at the beginning and end of the job and, secondly, that it allows connecting up by several operators, each one starting from a different angle, but with less difficulty than in the case of a patch with bars.

This operation is performed as follows: first of all the damaged panel is eliminated by two all-points cuts and two all-meshes cuts, each of them reaching the extreme end of the part to be removed; in order to eliminate the bars, the work is done in a continuous fashion, alternating cuts lengthwise and sidewise. Then from elsewhere, a suitable patch for the repair is taken out of a panel. The dimensions of the patch must be equal to those of the hole minus one mesh in height and in width.

After all knots on the free meshes of the tear and of the patch have been eliminated, they are joined together by a join.[1]

For the purpose the end of the twine is affixed by a single sheet bend onto the mesh of the left or the right corner of the upper edge of the tear leaving about 10 cm of unattached twine hanging.

Then the first mesh of one side of the patch is connected in the same way as a pick-up mesh. Then, one after another going all around, the other meshes of the upper edge and the points of the side edge are joined up, in the way indicated in the examples illustrating how horizontal and vertical tears are mended.

Once these two edges have been tied together the thread is cut about 10 cm from the last knot in order to be attached by a simple fisherman's knot to the free twine left hanging at the beginning of the operation. Then the two other edges are joined together and the operation is terminated by a flat knot tying the needle twine to the piece left unattached after the first part of the operation. The mesh side is then rebuilt just as would be done in terminating on a bar.

The insertion of the patch, here performed in two steps, can also be done in continuous fashion. It suffices, instead of cutting the thread off half way, to continue the connecting up of first the meshes along the lower edge and secondly the points of the other side edge, after turning the net upside down, or for a piece of netting that is not hung, in the inverse position.

Further on we will explain how a patch is inserted on the lower selvedge of the wing of a bottom trawl.

5.3 Repairs on selvedges other than those in the inner edges of wings

Such repairing is usually begun on the inside of the netting but always terminates on the selvedge itself. Thus, when the damage extends in several directions into the inside of the net, one first mends the various gaps so that

---

[1] The reader is reminded that "join" refers to the braiding of a row connecting two all-meshes cuts. The terms "crosswise join" and "lengthwise join" are used when the braided row respectively joins either meshes or points.

at the end one has only a single tear. At that point, the mending of this single tear and of the selvedge, if its trimming permits, is done in continuous fashion; otherwise this last part of the operation is performed in two steps, as we shall see later on. Here again we shall begin by the simplest cases and just as for the repairs of the oblique edges, with bating.

5.3.1   REPAIR OF AN ALL-MESHES EDGE

It will be assumed that the tear effects an edge consisting of meshes and extends several meshes in width and depth (Figure 46).

After trimming the special features will be: the starting bar at the upper portion; the end bar on the row immediately above the edge consisting of meshes to be repaired, from either the right or left side; one point on the other edge and at the same level as the end bar.

Mending is continued up to the next-to-last row, as in the case of an ordinary tear and is completed as follows.

Starting from the last point of the edge opposite the end bar, the meshes are braided toward the latter. One ends on the bar by forming a last mesh measured by pulling over the one or several fingers the mesh being made and the one at the base of the end bar.

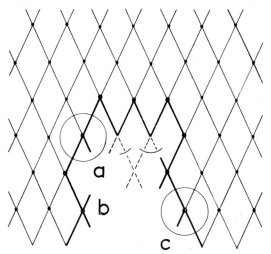

FIGURE 46.—Tear along an all-meshes selvedge. a—starting bar; b—side mesh marking the place where a start is made on rebuilding the selvedge; c—end bar.

5.3.2   REPAIR OF AN ALL-POINTS SELVEDGE

For this example only we shall describe two types of mending:

one starting on the selvedge when it is the only part torn (Figure 47);

the other, the most common one, when the tear of the selvedge also extends upward and inward into the panel; one then starts on the inside and at the highest portion of the break (Figure 48).

First case: after the hole has been trimmed, the starting and end bars will appear on the selvedge.

Immediately after starting on the bar, a first point is formed along the selvedge as well as the next ones on each return to the selvedge. One terminates on the end bar by making the last point.

Second case: mending starts in the inside of the panel where a bar is left at the upper portion. Then one mends the portion of the tear in the inside of the panel until one reaches the selvedge. At that point what follows immediately after the points that have not been destroyed is either a mesh (Figure 48A) or a bar (Figure 48B).

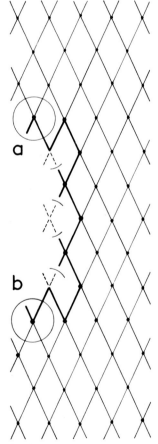

FIGURE 47.—Single tear on a selvedge consisting entirely of points.   a and b—starting and end bars along the selvedge.

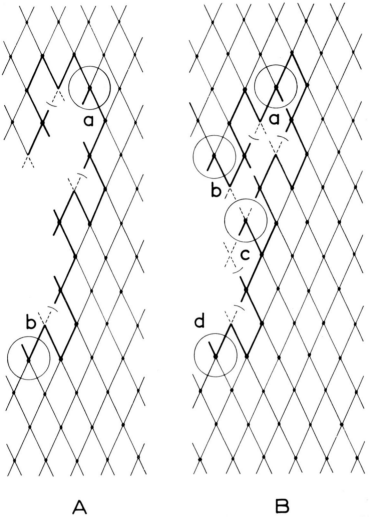

A   B

FIGURE 48.—Tear on all-points selvedge extending into the panel. A—a mesh follows the point that has not been destroyed, a and b—starting and end bars in continuous mending; B—a bar follows the point not destroyed, in two-step mending: a and b—starting and end bars for the first step; c and d—starting and end bars for the second step.

In the first case, the mesh allows for continuous mending. First of all one trims the side that leads to the lower portion of the tear in order to leave the end bar there, then the mending is continued by making the first point starting from the mesh; the next ones are braided as indicated for the repair of the preceding breach.

In the second case, continuous mending is not possible because of the presence of the bar. The first part of the repairing is stopped on this bar, to form a corner mesh which is, as will be remembered, both a mesh and a point. The trimming afterwards leaves a new starting bar at this level but on the side opposite the corner mesh and the finishing mesh at the inside of the hole. The conditions for mending are then the same as in the first instance.

When the tear extends a little into the inside, it is possible to start the trimming on the selvedge in order to leave a mesh that is essential for continuous mending.

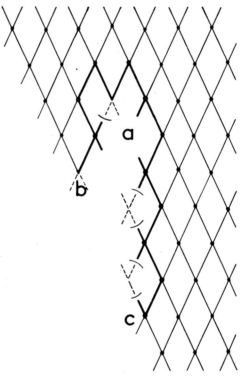

FIGURE 49.—Tear on all-bars selvedge. a and c—starting and finishing bars; b—mesh delimiting the tear on the selvedge, starting point for mending of a tear that does not extend further up into the inside of the netting.

5.3.3 MENDING OF AN ALL-BARS SELVEDGE

We shall use as an example a tear or an all-bars selvedge that extends upward into the netting

We shall describe how this mending is done starting from the inside of the netting and will indicate in this description the place where the repair would start in the case of a tear that did not affect the selvedge.

After trimming, the noticeable features will be: the starting bar at the upper portion of the breach and in the inside of the netting; one mesh at the intersection of one of the sides of the breach and the selvedge; one point at the lower level at the intersection of the other side of the breach and the selvedge (Figure 49).

The repair is done in the usual way until one reaches the mesh mentioned above. This mesh is the one from which the mending would start if the tear began at this level without reaching into the inside of the netting; from that point on, braiding is resumed toward the inside after making an initial pinched mesh.

Going back to the selvedge, the last mesh of the row is formed on the mesh and loop of the preceding row taken together as support.

It should be pointed out that these two steps correspond to the braiding of an all-bars piece with bating described in the preceding chapter (Figures 17 and 18).

To complete the process, the point at the lower level is connected by a piece of twine equal to two mesh sides to the last mesh made on which the double sheet bend for finishing also catches the said piece of twine.

5.3.4   Mending a selvedge consisting of one point and an even number of bars

We shall first describe, for purposes of illustration the mending of a selvedge braided or cut by one point—two bars cutting pattern, which will enable us to sum up the principles of repairing of all selvedges of the same type having an even number of bars. The components in this process will be remade in the same way as explained in the preceding chapter (Figure 19A and B).

Further on we shall indicate how mending of such edges and of those with points and an uneven number of bars is completed.

We will assume that the tear extends both into the inside and upward, starting from the selvedge and ruining it mainly downward. Thus the mending will be begun on the inside of the net and will be done either continuously, if in trimming it is possible to make initial point with a single piece of twine or, if not, in two steps.

Having left the starting bar inside the net, trimming will first be done to the point where the selvedge was broken. The noticeable features on the latter will be: either those of an entire process plus one bar that marks the beginning of the breach, or else some of the components of the process plus a mesh which, again, will indicate where the breach starts.

Thus one would have on the selvedge, starting from the preceding full process, one of the four sets of features now listed:

(1) the parts involved in the process plus a bar (in this case, one point—three bars);

(2) the point of the process plus one mesh;

(3) the point and one bar of the process plus a mesh;

(4) the parts involved in the process plus a mesh.

We point out that the trimming should not leave along the selvedge more than one bar in addition to those involved in the process. It is therefore necessary to eliminate any extra bars there may be.

In order to know during the mending whether the point is to be made of single or double twine, the intermediary knot is taken as the point of reference. This knot comes just before the point and consequently after the bars contained in the process. The intermediary knot is formed:

> either *starting* from the bar extra to those of the normal process, in this instance the third, in which case the next side mesh will be made of single twine;
>
> or else, *finishing* on this extra bar, or a loop as will be indicated further on, in which case the point is made of double twine.

The repair is made taking into account the component parts in the selvedge to complete the knots in the order just indicated.

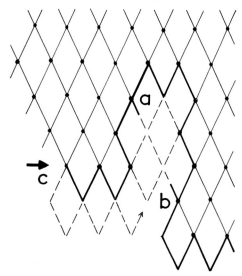

FIGURE 50.—Tear along a one point—two bars selvedge. The noticeable features are the parts of the normal process plus one bar. This extra bar is shown by the arrow. a and b—starting and finishing bars of the first step in the mending; c—extra bar that is used to start the second step of the mending.

Example No. 1. Special features: the process parts plus one bar (Figure 50).

Obviously here, starting with the third bar, both the intermediary knot and the point will be made of single twine.

The mending will be done first inside the net, stopping at the level of the row next to the selvedge, without braiding this row.

Once the twine has been cut, the third bar along the selvedge will be used to start the second step of the mending. It becomes the intermediary knot because of the making of the point which, it will be recalled, is made of a single piece of twine.

Following the braiding of the row that leads back to the selvedge, the mending is continued as shown in the next example after the second portion of the tear has been trimmed.

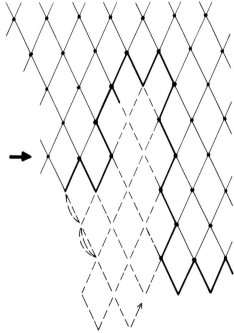

FIGURE 51.—Tear on a one point—two bars selvedge. The special features are the point of the process followed by a mesh. Mending is continuous from the starting bar on.

Example No. 2. Special features: the point of the process followed immediately by a mesh (Figure 51).

Mending of the inside portion of the net is done to the point where one reaches the selvedge where, by braiding the last mesh of the row, the first bar of the process is formed.

After the second portion of the tear is trimmed, braiding is done toward the inside, forming one pinched mesh at the start and then the second bar of the process.

On returning to the selvedge, the final mesh is made by taking together as a support the last mesh and the loop of the preceding row. From this point on, where the third bar just obtained, will become an intermediary knot, braiding is continued toward the inside starting with a single twine point.

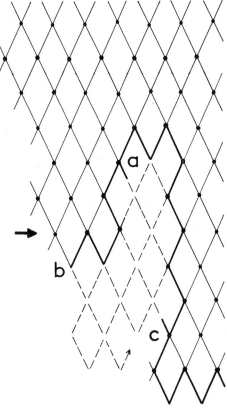

FIGURE 52.—Tear on a one point—two bars selvedge. The special features are the point and one bar of the process, shown by the arrow, plus a mesh; a—starting bar; b—mesh where the first step of the mending ends; c—starting bar for the second step of the mending.

The mending is then continued by repeating all phases of the operation again and again.

Example No. 3. Special features: the point and one bar of the process plus a mesh (Figure 52).

The bars here are again uneven in number so that the mending is done in two steps, as in example 1.

The mending of the first portion of the net is executed till one reaches the selvedge where the second bar of the process is made by braiding the first mesh of the row.

The second portion is trimmed and then the mending continues starting from a new bar left on the inside. By making the last mesh of the row along the selvedge, a bar is obtained that will become the intermediary knot when the point of single twine in the following row is formed.

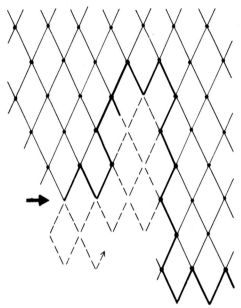

FIGURE 53.—Tear on a one point—two bars selvedge. The special features are the parts involved in the process plus one mesh. This mesh, shown by the arrow, permits continuous mending.

The mending goes forward by repetition of all sequential phases of example No. 2.

Example No. 4 Special features (Figure 53): those involved the process, plus one mesh.

Here again there is an even number of bars so that the mending is done continuously, as in example No. 2. Therefore the trimming will be done all at once.

The mending is executed in the inside of the net to the point of reaching the selvedge where braiding of the last mesh of the row forms a third bar. This brings one back to conditions analogous to those in the second part of mending in example No. 3.

5.3.5   MENDING OF A SELVEDGE CONSISTING OF A ONE POINT AND AN UNEVEN NUMBER OF BARS

By way of illustration we shall describe the mending of a selvedge braided or cut according to the one point-one bar cutting pattern. As in the preceding operation, the example will give us an occasion to sum up the principles underlying repair of all selvedges of the same type but with an uneven number of bars. The parts contained in this process will be rebuilt in the same way as explained in the chapter on braiding (Figure 20A and B).

Assuming that the tear looks like the preceding one, the mending is done continuously but starting with one bar in the inside of the net. The making of the point of the process, alternatively in single twine and then in double, does not call for two-step mending.

Having left the starting bar in the inside of the panel, the entire breach will be trimmed. We will then have as an edging and for starting of the entire preceding process, one of three sets of features now listed:

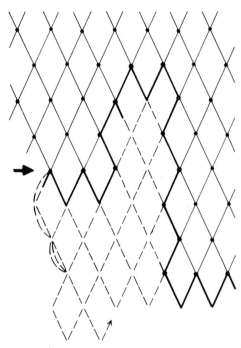

FIGURE 54.—Tear along a one point—one bar selvedge. The features are the parts for the process plus one bar. This bar, shown by the arrow, is the point of arrival of the first step of the mending and the point of start of the second portion. However the mending is continuous.

(1) the parts involved in the process plus a maximum of one bar (in this case one point-two bars);

(2) the point of the process followed immediately by a mesh;

(3) the parts contained in the process plus one mesh.

This time the knots along the selvedge will be, once the process is resumed: the knot of the point, one bar, the intermediary knot and the sequential repetition of these knots.

Mending will be performed as follows:

Example No. 1. Special features: the parts for the process plus one bar (Figure 54).

After mending has been finished in the inside of the net, a mesh is left that comes just before the extra bar.

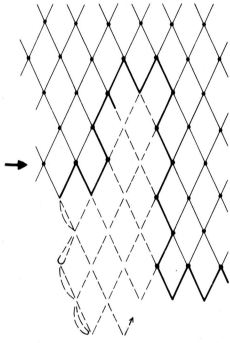

FIGURE 55.—Tear along a one point—one bar selvedge. The features are the point of the process, shown by the arrow, followed by a mesh. The mending is continuous but the points will be alternately in single and double twine.

A corner mesh is made by returning to the second bar that thus becomes an intermediary knot.

The braiding toward the inside begins with a pinched mesh. The result is that the point is doubled and a bar is formed at the level of the pinched mesh.

On returning to the selvedge, the last mesh of the row is made on the last mesh and loop of the preceding row taken together as a support, which leaves an extra bar; the point in single twine which is then braided changes this bar into an intermediary knot.

The mending then continues as described in the following example.

6*

Example No. 2: Special features: the point of the process followed immediately by one mesh (Fig. 55).

After mending of the inside of the net, one comes out at a mesh delimiting the gap in the selvedge. The braiding of the following row starts by a pinched mesh that leaves two bars, the second of which becomes the intermediary knot.

Returning to the selvedge the final mesh of the row is made on the loop taken by itself as a support, and then one works toward the inside. In this way the point is formed, that will be doubled by braiding a pinched mesh at the start.

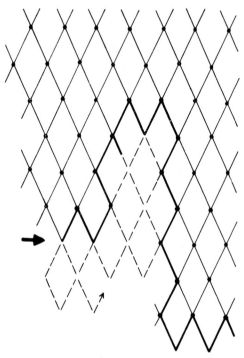

FIGURE 56.—Tear of one point—one bar selvedge. The special features are the parts used for the process plus one mesh. Mending is continuous, the mesh, shown by the arrow, becomes an intermediary knot and is followed by the single twine point. The points will then be alternately in single and double twine.

The mending continues by the repetition of the steps of example No. 1 following the making of the double twine point.

Example No. 3: Special features: those of the process plus one mesh (Figure 56).

In completing the mending of the inside of the net, one obtains a mesh as shown above, where an extra bar is formed. The single twine point, braided at the beginning of the following row, changes this bar into an intermediary knot.

The mending then goes forward by repetition of all the steps in example No. 2.

When three bars or more are involved in the process, they are made as indicated for braiding of selvedges with bating (Figures 17 and 18) up to the point where a point has to be made of either single or double twine.

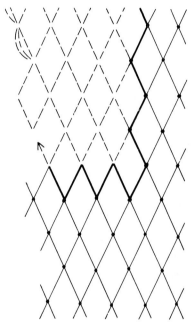

FIGURE 57.—End of the repair of a one point—one bar selvedge. The special features are the point of the process preceded by a mesh.

5.3.6.   END OF THE REPAIR ON SELVEDGES CONSISTING OF POINTS-AND-BARS

The repair of the breach is completed in several ways depending on the features of the selvedge along the lower portion.

(1) *The point of the process preceded by a mesh.* After this mesh is picked up to become the intermediary knot, the mending is completed on the last mesh of the preceding row (Figure 57). When in addition to this last one there is a loop, both of these are taken together.

(2) *The point of the process preceded by a bar.* In completing the braiding of the first row, the final part is made either on a mesh alone (Figure 58A) or else the mesh together with a loop, or else on a loop by itself if a double twine point is to be made (Figure 58B). From this point on, the bar is joined up to the end of a piece of twine equal to twice the length of the mesh sides

and ending up on the last mesh braided, by inserting into the double sheet bend the thread that connects up the bar.

(3) *A point outside the process which will become a bar.* The last mesh of the row that precedes the final row may or may not be combined with a loop. It will not be combined for a tear in a single row or when a single twine point for the process has just been formed. It will be accompanied by a loop in all other cases. This loop is taken together with the mesh, or separately, depending on the part or parts still to be made.

If the mesh and the loop are taken together, one will end on:

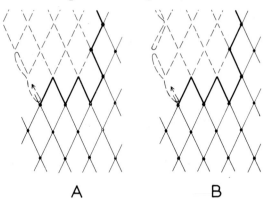

A   B

FIGURE 58.—End of repair on a point-and-bars selvedge. The special features are the point of the process preceded by a bar. A—making two bars; B—making one point, in double twine and one bar.

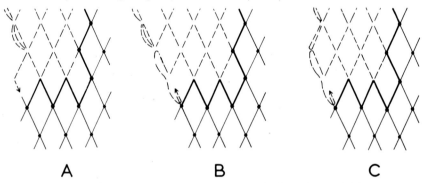

A   B   C

FIGURE 59.—End of the repair on a point-and-bars selvedge. The special features are a point (not that used in the process) preceded by a mesh. A—making the point of the process; B—making of three bars; C—making a point in double twine and two bars.

(1) either the knot of the existing point (Figure 59A); in this case the point of the process will be of a single twine;

(2) or on the last mesh braided of the end row (Figure 59B). This will leave three bars. The last mesh of the row is made by holding the mesh and the loop of the preceding row together. From this point on, the knot of the

point is tied with a length of twine equal to two sides of the mesh and one ends on the last mesh made, by tying the thread connecting the knot of the point into a double sheet bend.

If one takes the mesh and loops separately (Figure 59C), a point in double twine followed by two bars will be made. This is finished up in exactly the same way as in the preceding example.

5.4   Repairing the inner selvedges of the trawl wings

The reinforcement for the inner selvedges of the wings is braided with a double twine, in the case of a flymesh selvedge, but usually with a single piece of more resistant twine than for the wing if the selvedge involves braiding with batings.

Such a reinforcement averages in width of from one to five meshes along the entire depth of the wing except for one portion of the extremity of the fore where it is made the full width of the headpiece and on two to five meshes deep as well as on the far end, toward the corner of the wing where it takes on the shape of a triangle some 10 to 20 meshes wide by 8 to 10 meshes deep (Figure 60).

In order to braid such a reinforcement, the edge of the single-twine panel should have: a series of points necessary for braiding of the triangle at the back portion of the wing; alternating points and meshes, the tapering rate

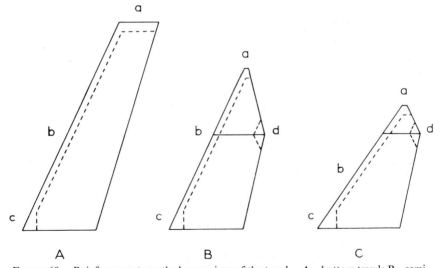

FIGURE 60.—Reinforcements on the lower wings of the trawl.   A—bottom trawl; B—semi-pelagic trawl; C—pelagic trawl; a—reinforcement of the headpiece or the tip of the wing; b—reinforcement of the inner selvedge; c—triangular reinforcement at the corner; d—rhomboid-shaped reinforcement at the junction of the headpieces.

being equal to that of the selvedge to be made; meshes for braiding of the headpiece. Further on we shall see (Chapter D. 1) how to begin the reinforcement to avoid any discrepancy as the process continues.

In the workshop, mending of these selvedges is done in the direction of tapering and in two distinct parts: first the plain panel and then the reinforcement. Depending on the type of selvedge, the trimming and mending of the nonreinforced panel is differentiated only by the number of meshes to be left along the edge. These appear in the alternation established depending on the taper ratio. In this ratio, the figure in the numerator indicates the number of meshes to be distributed in relation to the number of points corresponding to the figure in the denominator (Table 1).

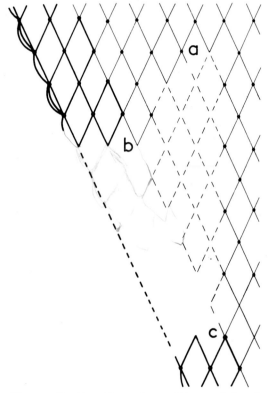

FIGURE 61.—Repairing of an all-bars reinforced selvedge. a—starting bar; b—single-twine mesh left free during mending; c—end bar.

We shall assume in each example that we have to mend a tear located in the central portion of the wing, which breaks the selvedge toward the bottom and also extends upwards into the inside of the panel. First of all it is necessary to do the trimming and mending of the tear in the single-twine piece and then, as a second step to trim the reinforced selvedge leaving no bar except for flymesh selvedges in which a starting and end bar are necessary.

In the first of the four examples of repairing we will describe, we will explain how the two parts of the net are trimmed and mended. In the other three examples, we will indicate only what alternation is needed along the edge of the non-reinforced panel before explaining how the reinforced selvedge is to be mended.

5.4.1 REPAIRING OF ALL-BARS AND FLYMESHES SELVEDGES WITH A TAPER RATIO $R = 1/1$

It is by braiding the reinforcements that the all-bars selvedges are formed in the inside of the wings. This braiding is done starting with alternation of one point and one mesh, the remaking of which by mending we will have to describe, as the repairing of such a selvedge and the way it is started has already been explained. This alternation corresponds to the all-bars tapering rate by which one braids reinforced selvedges with batings and flymeshes.

Mending of the non-reinforced panel. The tear is trimmed to the point where the reinforcement is broken, there being two possible cases.

(1) *The last component brought out is a single-twine mesh* (Figure 61). The trimming of the other side of the tear can be completed immediately and the repairing itself is performed as follows.

From the starting bar, one mends until one makes a mesh that precedes the one indicated above. The latter is left free and then one braids towards the inside, marking the point by an overhand knot. This phase of the operation is then repeated again and again on each return to the edge and ends on the bar that joins two double-twine and one single-twine meshes.

(2) *The last component obtained is a bar* (Figure 62). One trims the other side of the tear to a sufficient depth to be able to carry out the first part of the mending that one stops on the bar by forming a mesh. The twine is then cut and the trimming is completed, leaving another starting bar in the

TABLE 1—ALTERNATION OF POINTS AND MESHES ON EDGES OF THE WINGS IN SINGLE TWINE, EXCEPT FOR THE TIPS, TO BE USED AS SUPPORT IN BRAIDING REINFORCED SELVEDGES IN MESHES AND BARS AT AN EQUIVALENT TAPER RATIO. THE SYMBOLS USED B, T AND N ARE THOSE OF THE ISO. B = ON THE BIAS : BAR; N = NORMAL : POINT; T = TRANSVERSAL : MESH.

Reinforced selvedges	Taper ratio	Alternation of points and meshes
All B[1]	$R = 1/1$	1N 1T
2B 1T[1]	2/1	1N 2T
3B 1T	5/3	twice 1N 2T, once 1N 1T
4B 1T	3/2	once 1N 2T, once 1N 1T
5B 1T	7/5	twice 1N 2T, 3 times 1N 1T
6B 1T	4/3	once 1N 2T, twice 1N 1T
7B 1T	9/7	twice 1N 2T, 5 times 1N 1T
8B 1T	5/4	once 1N 2T, 3 times 1N 1T
9B 1T	11/9	twice 1N 2T, 7 times 1N 1T
10B 1T	6/5	once 1N 2T, 4 times 1N 1T

[1] Or flymesh selvedges

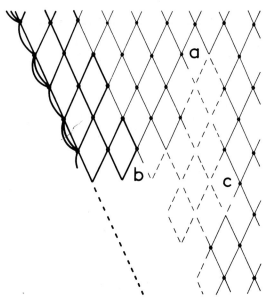

FIGURE 62.—Mending of an all-bars reinforced selvedge. Case of a two-steps mending: a and b starting and finishing bars of the first step; c—starting bar of the second step.

inside. The second part of the mending is performed as indicated above.

Mending of a flymesh selvedge. To simplify the description of this mending process, we shall assume that after the trimming of the reinforcement, there is at the two ends of the tear a large, intact mesh (Figure 63): the one on the upper portion will be followed by the starting bar and the one, on the lower portion, will be preceded by the finishing bar.

The mending is done as follows:

> from the starting bar, one row is braided toward the inside and then another toward the selvedge;
> in the following row, one flymesh is made at the start and then one continues in the same fashion as explained in the last chapter (Figure 27);
> once a last flymesh has been made, the repairing ends on the finishing bar.

5.4.2   REPAIRING OF A FLYMESH SELVEDGE, TAPER RATIO $R = 2/1$

In this instance, the edge of the small non-reinforced panel will have one point alternating with two meshes.

The repairing is executed in exactly the same way as explained in the last operation, except for the two following points:

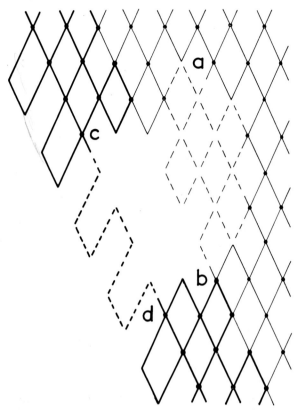

FIGURE 63.—Repairing a flymesh selvedge ($R = 1/1$).
a and b—starting and finishing bars of the mending in
single twine; c and d—starting and finishing bars of
the mending in double twine.

(1) In mending the single twine panel: two meshes instead of one are left
on each return of the edge (Figure 64);

(2) In braiding the reinforced selvedge: the flymeshes are made on the
two meshes of the preceding row taken as a support (Figure 28).

5.4.3   MENDING OF A SELVEDGE CONSISTING OF ONE MESH AND AN EVEN NUMBER OF BARS

We will use as an example the mending of a one mesh-two bars selvedge
at a taper ratio of $R = 2/1$.

The trimming and mending of the non-reinforced portion of the net are
performed exactly as in the last operation, the selvedge being formed with
the same taper.

Mending the reinforced portion. After the trimming, the mesh of the
process delimits the nondestroyed portion of the selvedge, on both the upper

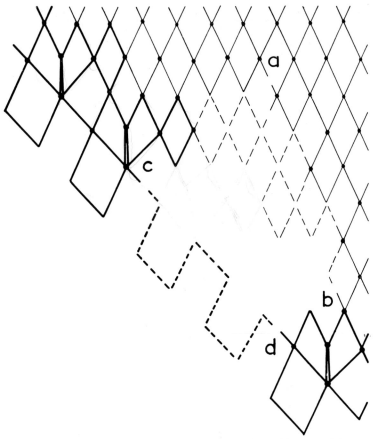

FIGURE 64.—Repairing of a flymesh selvedge ($R = 2/1$). a and b—
starting and finishing bars for single twine mending; c and d—starting
and finishing bars for double twine mending.

and lower sides. At this last level, the lower side, it is preceded by a point.

Mending is begun on the upper side, on the intermediary knot between the mesh of the process and the next mesh (Figure 65). On the latter a pinched mesh is made by braiding toward the inside, then one continues as indicated in the last chapter (Figure 21 A and B).

To finish, when the meshes of the lower side have been picked up, two meshes are braided, the last being doubled. One joins the point by a length of twine equal to two mesh sides and ends on the next to last mesh made by inserting the thread that ties in the point into the double sheet bend (Figure 66).

When the reinforced selvedge to be remade involves an even number of bars, but more than two, the repair, depending on the place where the selvedge has been broken, begins either on the intermediary knot as has just been explained, or else on one of the even number bars and in this case a pinched mesh is also found on the following mesh.

At the end of this repair, if the special feature is a point preceding a bar, the process is finished in exactly the same way as in repairing an all-bars selvedge.

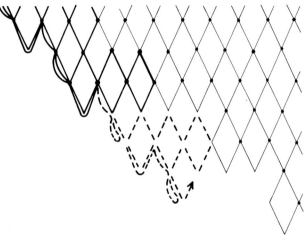

FIGURE 65.—Repairing a selvedge of one mesh and an even number of bars pattern.

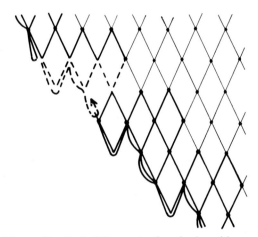

FIGURE 66.—End of the repair of a selvedge with one mesh and an even number of bars.

In pelagic trawls, the two bars-one mesh process of braiding is often used in order to make the back end of the wing toward its corner. In such a case the single twine edge of the wing that serves as a support is made either of all points or of meshes and points combined.

5.4.4   Repairing of a selvedge consisting of a one mesh and an uneven number of bars pattern

We shall first describe how one mends selvedges consisting of more than one bar and will explain at the end of the operation how a selvedge of a one bar-one mesh pattern is done.

Trimming and mending of the nonreinforced portions are done as we have already explained in preceding operations, but the edge is formed by the alternating point and mesh as appropriate for the reinforcement braiding.

After the trimming of the latter, the parts involved in the process, which delimit the nondestroyed portion of the selvedge are: first on the upper side of the hole, the last bar and the mesh, which always go together, or one of the other bars; secondly, on the lower side of the gap, one or more of the parts used in the process except for the first bar, preceded each time by one point.

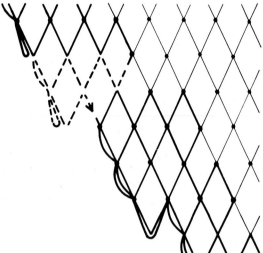

Figure 67.—End of the repair of a selvedge with one mesh and an uneven number of bars.

Depending upon the point where the selvedge is broken, the mending starts either on the intermediary knot, as in the preceding operation, or on any one of the bars except the last.

Whatever the starting point, one pinched mesh is first made and this begins, continues or ends the series of bars involved in the process. Consequently, three possible cases may occur after the first row has been braided:

(1) at least two bars are missing: in this case one braids toward the selvedge, then toward the inside, as in the all-bars braiding (Figure 18B).

(2) only one bar has to be made: one row is built, the terminal bar of

which on the selvedge is formed on the mesh and loop of the preceding row taken together; then one doubles the last mesh obtained as indicated in the last chapter (Figure 21A):

(3) the last bar and the mesh have just been made: these parts are left free in returning to the selvedge.

After each braiding toward the inside, the mending is continued by repeating whichever one of the three above-described phases as appropriate.

At the end of the mending the meshes are picked up in the last row and the process is completed as follows:

(1) the last two bars and the single twine mesh of the process will have to be made: after having picked up the one or more meshes, the braiding is continued toward the selvedge to form the next-to-last bar. One pinched mesh and then the mesh of the process are formed before ending on the point (Figure 67).

(2) At least three bars have to be obtained: the mending is ended as in the finish of the all-bars selvedges.

(3) The doubled mesh and the two first bars of the process have to be formed: the mending is completed as in the preceding operation (Figure 66).

Selvedges consisting of one bar-one mesh and two bars-one mesh have, after trimming, the same features.

When the tear effects only the triangular reinforcement, mending can start either on the selvedge or inside the net. In the first place, one begins on the intermediary knot after the free mesh of the process to form a pinched mesh at the start; then one makes the selvedge as described in the last chapter (Figures 21 and 22). In the second case, the mesh of the process is left, then the last mesh braided is doubled and the work continues as though the start had been made on selvedge.

The repair is completed in the manner that will be indicated further on in the making of wing corners (Figure 78).

5.5   Other repairs with bating

We shall describe two last examples of repairs with bating made either in the workshop or on board ship.

5.5.1   INSERTING A PATCH ON THE INNER SELVEDGE OF A LOWER WING OF A BOTTOM TRAWL

The replacement of a strip of netting from 10 to 15 meshes deep into this vunerable portion of the trawl frequently has to be done on board ship as well as in the workshop, when a wornout or deformed piece of netting needs to be changed. We shall assume here that this operation needs to be done in the central portion of the wing.

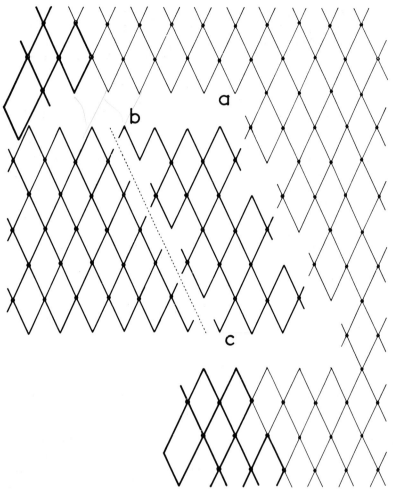

FIGURE 68.—Inserting of a patch on the inner selvedge of a lower wing of a bottom trawl. a to b—Joining the upper edge of the patch; a to c—Fixing the side edge and the lower edge of the patch. The dotted line shows the cut made after the patch has been inserted.

The trimming of the hole where the patch is to be inserted is done as follows:

Starting from the upper part of the damaged portion, the following steps are executed: a bar on the intermediary knot that follows the flymesh at this point; a number of meshes sufficient for the elimination of the panel to be replaced; a one point-one mesh cut parallel to the edge and down to the lower level of the damaged portion where the cut ends in a point; one all-meshes cut going toward the selvedge (Figure 68). The trimming is completed by one bar formed on the intermediary knot that precedes the flymesh marking the end point of the break in the selvedge.

The patch is taken from a netting panel involving an upper edge all in meshes and a one point-one mesh cut parallel to the one on the wing.

Repair begins with the linking up, along the upper side, of meshes of the gap and the patch in the following manner.

A simple sheet bend is made in the thread at about 10 cm from its end on the mesh that marks the inside corner of the gap. The joint is brought as far as the next-to-last single twine mesh of the hole and one ends on the mesh after the patch.

Once the thread has been cut and tied up to the free and left at the start, the linking up of the two edges consisting of points and meshes continues, as in the repair of an oblique tear, making the join at the lower portion of single twine meshes. The operation ends on one mesh of the patch after the first mesh in double twine one comes across has been picked up.

The alternation of one point and one mesh necessary for braiding of the reinforcement and of the flymeshes is established when the patch is cut to measure, parallel to the selvedge (see legend Figure 68).

At the edge, when quick repair is necessary, only the flymeshes are braided in double twine. In this case the joins are extended to the upper and lower portions as far as the selvedge, before they end on the patch, as above. Furthermore, the join at the lower level is followed by braiding in one extra mesh on the patch to start the alternation of one point-one mesh along the selvedge in single twine.

5.5.2. REPAIR OF A PIECE OF NETTING SEPARATED CROSSWISE

The repair of a piece of netting that has been cut across in two parts when damaged is done in two steps. One begins on either one or another of the side selvedges by preliminary work that professionals call the "making of a control" that consists of remaking one of the selvedges and the exact depth of the piece, on a limited width, either by braiding or with a patch. After which the tear is mended in the same way as a tear ending on the selvedge.

In this operation we shall describe only how a braided control is made and then stipulate in what cases and how this work is done using a patch.

As an illustration we shall take a lower wing of the bottom trawl damaged as described above. We shall assume that it is the central portion that was damaged and that conditions are favourable for braiding the control, that will be done here on the flymesh selvedge (Figure 69).

It should be reiterated that two rows are necessary for the braiding of one flymesh. The height of the wing mounted on the trawl is therefore equal to the number of flymeshes.

Trimming is done as in the preceding operation, except for the two following points:

(1) on the portion of the wing where it is possible to work with baiting, a sufficient number of meshes are formed to braid the control; this

number must be at least equal to the number of flymeshes to be remade plus one; this figure is found by deducting the number of meshes remaining in each portion of the wing from the total number for the intact wing;

(2) on the other portion of the wing; only two or three meshes are trimmed along the selvedge, including the one formed from the intermediary knot just before the last flymesh.

FIGURE 69.—Braiding a control piece.

The flymeshes that are missing will be rebuilt as the braiding of each return to the selvedge progresses, whereas toward the inside this control is limited by the points. The number of meshes used as a support for this braiding is calculated during trimming. When all the flymeshes have been remade, the meshes are picked up, beginning with the first flymesh that has not been undone.

A patch is used to make the control, particularly when it is not possible to trim a sufficient number of meshes to provide support for the braiding with bating, or when there are too many meshes to be braided.

On a selvedge identical with the one in the preceding example, a control is also built with the help of a patch, as follows (Figure 70).

Trimming is done as explained above but forming at least two single-twine meshes on the portion of the wing set-up for braiding the reinforcement with bating; then one counts the number of meshes deep of the two portions of the wing;

the control section is made out of a netting strip in single twine of sufficient width and equal in depth to the number of flymeshes to be remade *minus one half-mesh* comprising a side edge cut on an all-bars pattern;

this cut edge is lined up parallel to the wing selvedge; the mesh along the selvedge of the patch is joined to the second mesh of single twine of the wing and then one joins up several meshes, working inwards;

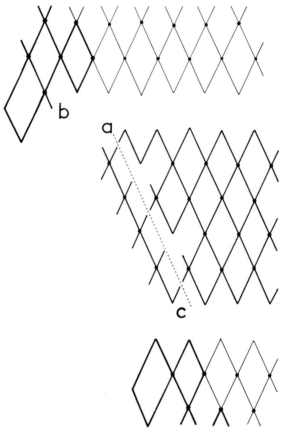

FIGURE 70.—Making a control piece using a patch. a—start of the join of the patch; b—starting bar for the double twine braiding; c—end of double twine braiding after the second portion of the wing has been connected up. The dotted line shows the cut made after the control piece has been inserted.

starting from the first fixed mesh of the patch, one makes a one point-one mesh cut to serve as a support for the double-twine reinforcement then made. Finally the other portion of the wing is connected up as described in the preceding example.

The width of the control is usually delimited during mending of the tear that follows making of the latter.

When the panel has neither flymeshes nor doubling, or, generally speaking, if one is working on outer selvedges of the sections of a trawl, it is not necessary to leave a bar in the trimmed portion. The number of meshes in depth of the control is in this case equal to that of the meshes to be remade minus one, and the first join is made starting from the selvedge. Once this phase of the operation has been completed, one continues on the control the sidewise cut of the panel before mending the second portion which is done starting from the selvedge. From this connection on, three possible cases can be considered, viz:

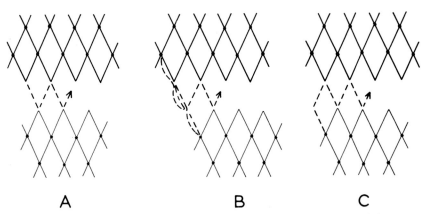

            A   **B**   **C**

FIGURE 71.—Lower join of a patch used as a control on a selvedge without reinforcement and flymesh. A—one bar still has to be made; B—three bars have to be made; C—one point and one bar still have to be made.

(1) A single bar is missing: the meshes are joined up starting from the first mesh of the control (Figure 71A).

(2) Three bars must be obtained: the last knot on the selvedge of the control is the starting point for the making of a pinched mesh on the next mesh. Then one joins up one after another: the knot of the point of the panel with a length of twine equal to two mesh sides; the loop of the pinched mesh, by inserting into the sheet bend the twine used to tie up the point and, finally, the second mesh of the control. The join is later extended inward (Figure 71B).

(3) One point plus one bar still have to be formed: one begins on the knot of the point of the panel and joins up the first mesh of the control by a length of twine equal to two mesh sides. From this point on the first mesh of the wing is picked up and the join is completed (Figure 71C).

5.6.   Repairs of flymesh selvedges, with increase

The repair of flymesh selvedges with increase is not generally done on board ship unless conditions are favourable. Each flymesh is then made starting from staplings used as support points

It should be remembered that staplings are loops formed by a double hanging twine connecting the flymeshes either to the groundrope bolchline, in the lower wings, or directly to the headline or to an intermediary line, in the upper wings.

We shall revert later on to the examples of tears chosen to explain how flymesh selvedges are mended with bating (Figures 63 and 64) and will only describe here how to make these large meshes with increase. Otherwise, all phases of the repair are the same, whether bating or increasing.

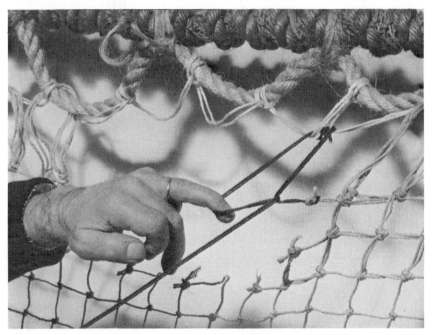

FIGURE 72.—Making the flymesh on a mesh.   A—measuring the flymesh before making it.

5.6.1   MAKING THE FLYMESH ON A MESH

Once the twine has been tied onto the starting bar, the needle is inserted into the stapling which already supports the preceding flymesh and then pulled out in the next one. With the left hand the twine is held in two places, first, at the place where the needle comes out of the stapling and, secondly, between the thumb and the index finger at a distance equal to a mesh side from the bar. The needle is passed behind that portion of the twine held

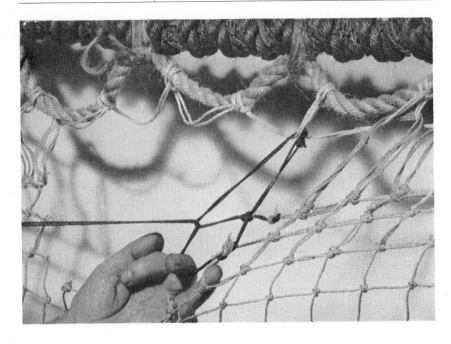

FIGURE 72 (*continued*).—Making the flymesh on a mesh.   B (*above*)—making the second knot; C (*below*): repair completed.

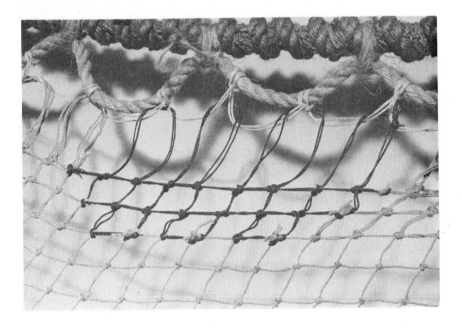

between the thumb and the index finger, as though one were going through a mesh in braiding. The size of the flymesh and the length of the mesh side are adjusted by sight (Figure 72A), after which a simple sheet bend is made on both sides of the angle formed by the twine starting from the bar. The flymesh, partly attached by this first knot, will then be permanently attached by a second one at the end of the braiding of the two rows (Figure 72B).

Then braiding is continued toward the inside and one again toward the selvedge, where the flymesh is taken as a support for making the last mesh of the row. The same conditions as at the start occur at the end of this phase of the operation, this operation being repeated as many times as there are flymeshes to be made. The operation is ended on the finishing bar after formation of the second knot that fixes the last mesh (Figure 72C).

5.6.2 MAKING OF THE FLYMESH ON TWO MESHES

The flymeshes are made as in the preceding operation, with the following added two details:

(1) when the flymesh is fixed by a first knot, a loop one half mesh in size is also made on the same support (Figure 73A);
(2) in returning to the selvedge, the next-to-last mesh of the row is braided on the loop only, used as a support (Figure 73B), and then the flymesh is fixed by a second knot formed at a distance equal to one mesh side (Figure 72B).

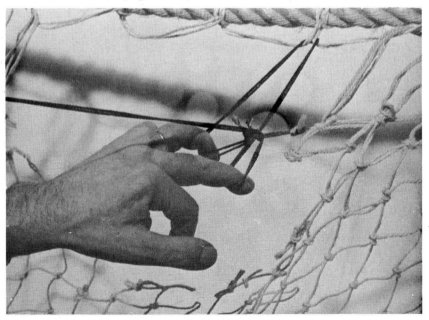

FIGURE 73.—Making the flymesh on two meshes. A—making the loop.

FIGURE 73 (*continued*).—Making of a flymesh on two meshes.   B—forming the next-to-last mesh. The second knot that will fix the flymesh will also form the last mesh.

CHAPTER 6

NOTES ON THE MAKING AND MOUNTING OF NET SECTIONS

6.1 Reinforcement braiding

This operation performed with bating on a headpiece is started by braiding of the triangle located at the level of the corner of the wing. One starts either from the side of the selvedge, flymeshes have to be made, or on a bar left in the single-twine panel for selvedges consisting of one mesh and an even number of bars. This last method makes it possible to double each time the mesh involved in the process; by beginning from the other side, that is to say from the side of the selvedge, the latter is made of single twine and a loop from one end to the other.

In the case of selvedges consisting of all-bars or of one mesh and an uneven number of bars, it is possible to begin braiding from either one side or the other, indifferently.

The wings of semi-pelagic and pelagic trawls have, in addition, a reinforcement, usually rhomboid-shaped, at the level of the junction of the wing lines, the width being from six to ten meshes. This is made by braiding a rhomboid identical to the one already cut out in the single-twine panel (Figure 60d).

We moreover mention the reinforcement of the forward edge of the belly consisting of a strip of double braided netting, averaging five meshes in depth, the width being usually equal to that of the panel.

6.2 Assembling the net sections

The various pieces of netting making up the fishing gear are assembled by two types of linkage which, it should be remembered, consist on the one hand of joins, requiring the braiding of an extra row, and on the other hand of seams, in which one or several meshes on the edge of each panel are joined together by a sort of braiding.

6.2.1 JOINS

Each join begins and ends at the extremities of the rear edge of the pieces and the connecting row, already counted off during construction, completes the depth and possibly the final width. This connection is made mesh by mesh when the two edges to be joined have the same number of meshes or else with take-up meshes in the opposite case.

Joins with take-up meshes

Two pieces of netting of the same width but of different meshsize will not have the same number of meshes. When such pieces are joined together, the additional or "take-up" meshes that are found on the panel of smaller meshsize therefore have to be interspersed among the meshes of the other panel in regular fashion. In order to determine the correct way of alternating or repeating in such take-up, the reader is referred to the work of C. Nédélec and L. Libert (*Le chalut*), p. 18.

These joins have to be made in trawl nets in several different ways, but whatever the case the meshes picked up are always those of the panel with the largest number of meshes and which, in working, is placed below the panel with the large meshes.

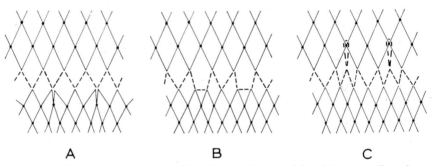

A   B   C

FIGURE 74.—Join of two panels in a 2/3 take-up ratio. A—join with two small meshes tied up together; B—join with braiding through the small meshes; C—join with extra loops on the large meshes.

Two of the smaller meshes are tied up with a knot by the twine used for joining them between two meshes of the upper panel (Figure 74A). This method is not the best because the force of traction on the panel will not be spread evenly.

All the meshes of the lower net are merely braided. Where there are take-up meshes, the twine is passed through two of them, but is knotted only on each mesh of the upper panel (Figure 74B). This type of join is used essentially on trawls for fast joining up of the extension piece to the body of the net and for insertion of protection pieces; the strain is spread better although slipping may cause premature abrasion of the loose meshes.

An extra loop is formed between two large meshes to be used as a support for the extra mesh to be picked up (Figure 74C). This loop is made as follows:

> when the mesh that comes before the take-up mesh is picked up the needle is passed through the next-to-last row of large meshes so as to skip over the knot after the last fixed mesh; the twine is tightened

FIGURE 75.—Joining up of panels with extra loops. A (*above*)—position of the index finger at the place where the side knot will be made; B (*below*)—holding two pieces of twine in position.

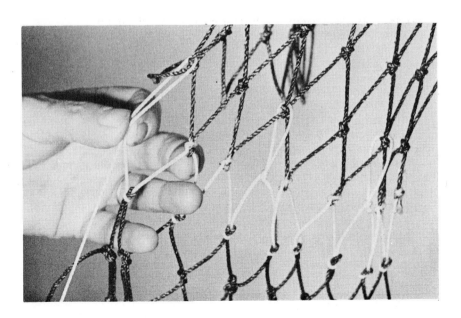

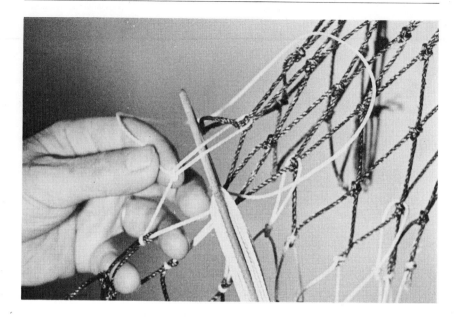

FIGURE 75 (*continued*).—Joining up two panels with extra loops.   C (*above*)—making the side knot; D (*below*)—linking up the take-up meshes.

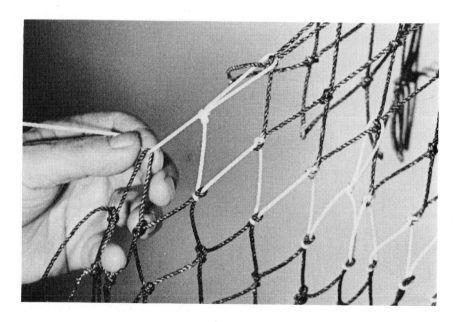

by holding the lower panel, and the place where the loop is to be fixed is marked by the index finger placed under the twine going toward the intermediary knot (Figure 75A);
the two pieces of twine are held tight between the index finger and the thumb placed on top (Figure 75B);
at this place the side knot closing the loop is made (Figure 75C);
and finally, the mesh to be taken up is picked up (Figure 75D).

This type of join is recommended for its good grip and its homogeneous distribution of the traction force.

Finishing joins at the wing corners

The corners of wings are made by braiding the extra components of the inner selvedges of the wings at the end of the join. Depending on the type of selvedge, the making of these components requires, first, braiding of one to three meshes on to the square piece, for the upper wings, or on the belly piece, for the lower wings.

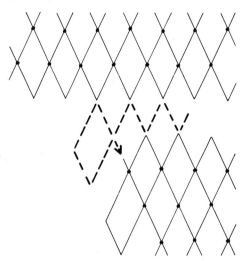

FIGURE 76.—Making the wing corner with a flymesh selvedge ($R = 1/1$).

(1) Flymesh selvedges: after the last mesh of the wing has been picked up, an extra one is braided on to it for use as a support for the flymesh and then one terminates on the bar (Figure 76). If the flymesh has to be formed on two meshes taken together, two of them are braided instead of one (Figure 77).

(2) All-bars selvedges: after the join is made, one mesh is braided and the point connected by lengths of twine equal to two mesh sides. One ends on the extra mesh by inserting the twine that connects the point into the double net knot (Figure 78).

(3) Two bars-one mesh selvedges: two meshes are formed after the join

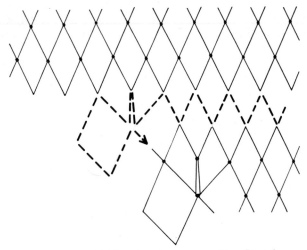

FIGURE 77.—Making the wing corner with a flymesh selvedge ($R = 2/1$).

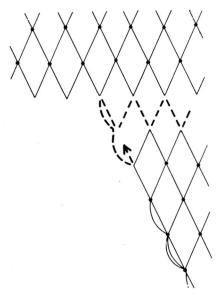

FIGURE 78.—Making the wing corner with an all-bars selvedge.

and then one mesh is pinched together onto the second. The point of the wing is rejoined after the mesh of the process has been made on the first extra mesh (Figure 78).

(4) One bar-one mesh selvedges; three meshes are braided after the join and the last is doubled. After which one mesh is pinched onto the second braided mesh and one ends as one does for the last selvedge (Figure 80).

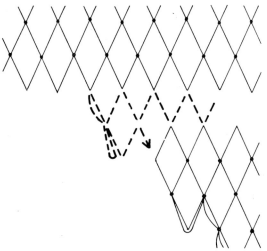

FIGURE 79.—Making the wing corner with a two bars—one mesh selvedge.

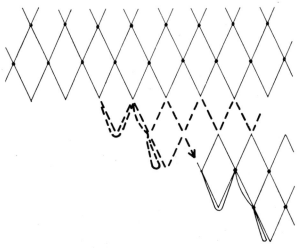

FIGURE 80.—Making the wing corner with a one bar-one mesh selvedge.

For all the selvedges made of meshes and bars equal in number to, or over, three, the procedure is the same as for an all-bars selvedge (Figure 78). In constructing corners of wings for one of these selvedges, three successive bars are formed; it is advisable to take them into account in braiding the reinforced triangle before making the join of the net section. For instance, selvedges made by the process using four, five or six bars and one mesh will each begin by one, two or three bars and one mesh.

6.2.2 SEAMS

With some exceptions, no seams are used in working on trawls except for assembling corresponding pieces of two panels to be joined. They are made by taking together three to six meshes on each edge to be sewn, one after another in regular fashion. When these edges have different cutting angles, it is best to work by counting off an equal number of knots to be sewn in along each edge. The operation, which is generally done with double twine, calls for a seizing with half hitches approximately every 50 cm, after four or five passages of the twine through the meshes. When this seam is not followed by mounting on a line, it can be made of quadruple twine to form a more uniform panel flange. In some instances, particularly when it is not desirable to have a visible line, a reinforcement rope is sewn in.

On board ship, sometimes a patch is inserted or a tear is repaired by uniting the edges to be joined by a loose seam with only very widely spaced seizings. This operation, usually called "lacing" can only be considered an exceptional and temporary measure; it can only be used when there is no danger of spoiling good trawl functioning.

CHAPTER 7

CONCLUSIONS

Mending is a specialized skilled technique in fishing evidenced by the fact that the rating of "netmender" and "chief netmender" indicates some promotion up the vocational ladder. In fact, the handling of all problems of net repair in the minimum amount of times requires quick comprehension and accurate execution of the mending, which can only be the result of very thorough apprenticeship and long experience.

Despite overall advances in technology, we believe that mending and the teaching of this art will certainly continue to be necessary because fishing gear consisting of net panels or sections and particularly trawls, will always get torn. Nevertheless, obviously, the use of synthetic materials and new types of gear will tend to prolong their useful life; that is why when very large tears occur, fishermen are apt to discard and change a whole panel, or even a whole net, especially in industrial fisheries.

Despite this trend, certain mending operations will always have to be done on board ship as for instance, repairing of small tears or insertion of patches, which operations are not very easy to perform as we have seen. Mending in its present form will therefore be needed for many years to come both in small-scale fisheries and in the workshops where nets are made and repaired and where very often work done hastily at sea has to be redone. The future of this speciality obviously depends on the teaching of the technique for which optimum conditions exist only in seamen's apprentice-ship schools.

We therefore believe that this handbook in which both traditional style mending and details of recent practices have been described, will be very useful for all who want to be able to tackle problems involved in net mending.

BIBLIOGRAPHIC REFERENCES

For further information on certain details or technical terms, the reader is referred to the following works:

BRANDT (A. VON), 1957.   Fischnetzknoten. Aus der Geschichte der Fischnetzherstellung. Schriften der Bunderforschungsanstalt für Fischerei, 2, 66 p.

EITZEN (J. H. C. VON), 1960.   Schleppnetze in der Hochseefischerei, *Ibid.*, 4, 182.

GARNER (J.), 1956.   *Deep sea trawling*. The Gourock Ropework Co. Ltd.

—— 1960.   *How to make and set nets*. London, Fishing News (Books) Ltd. Edit.

HODSON (A.) 1964.   *Introduction to trawling. Ibid.*

NÉDÉLEC (C.) and LIBERT (L.) 1964.   Le Chalut—Paris, Institut des Pêches marit., Edit.

OLIVIER (R. C.), 1965.   *Trawlermen's handbook*. London, Fishing News (Books) Ltd., Edit.

PERCIER (A.), 1958.   *Les specifications des engins de pêche*. Rev. Trav. Inst. Pêches Marit., 22 (1), pp. 7–30.

VANNETELLE (L.), 1939.   *Fabrication et emploi des filets de pêche*. Paris, Gauthier-Villars, Edit.

Other books published by
Fishing News Books Ltd

Free catalogue available on request

Advances in aquaculture
Advances in fish science and technology
Aquaculture practices in Taiwan
Atlantic salmon: its future
Better angling with simple science
British freshwater fishes
Commercial fishing methods
Control of fish quality
Culture of bivalve molluscs
Echo sounding and sonar for fishing
The edible crab and its fishery in British waters
Eel capture, culture, processing and marketing
Eel culture
European inland water fish: a multilingual catalogue
FAO catalogue of fishing gear designs
FAO catalogue of small scale fishing gear
FAO investigates ferro-cement fishing craft
Farming the edge of the sea
Fish and shellfish farming in coastal waters
Fish catching methods of the world
Fisheries of Australia
Fisheries oceanography and ecology
Fishermen's handbook
Fishery products
Fishing boats and their equipment
Fishing boats of the world 1
Fishing boats of the world 2
Fishing boats of the world 3
The fishing cadet's handbook
Fishing ports and markets
Fishing with electricity
Fishing with light
Freezing and irradiation of fish
Handbook of trout and salmon diseases
Handy medical guide for seafarers: fishermen,
    trawlermen and yachtsmen
How to make and set nets
Inshore fishing: its skills, risks, rewards